transformation journal

A DAILY WALK
IN THE
WORD

Edited by
Sue Nilson Kibbey,
Carolyn Slaughter,
and
Kevin Applegate

Abingdon Press
Nashville

This book is printed on acid-free paper.

Library of Congress Cataloging-in-Publication Data

Transformation journal : a daily walk in the Word / edited by Sue
Nilson Kibbey and Carolyn Slaughter.
      p. cm.
 Originally published: Nashville, TN: Abingdon Press, 2007.
 ISBN: 978-0-687-65502-1 (pbk. : alk. paper)
1. Bible—Meditations.   2. Devotional calendars.   I. Kibbey, Sue
Nilson.   II. Slaughter, Carolyn, 1949–
    BS491.5.T73   2008
    242′.2—dc22

                                                    2008035561

08 09 10 11 12 13 14 15 16 17—10 9 8 7 6 5 4 3 2 1
MANUFACTURED IN CHINA

INTRODUCTION

This life *Transformation Journal* (TJ) is created, designed, and written with the passionate desire to help you grow in your relationship with God as you walk with God's word each day.

As you use this journal, you will explore fifty-two different topics that will be part of God's plan for transformation in your life. Through your daily walk with the word, you will interact with selected Scriptures, grasp God's truths, and apply those truths to your life. By the end of one year you will have experienced God's personal interest and investment in you, learned about God's will for you, and be equipped to extend your growth as a disciple as you continue your spiritual journey.

By spending a full week reading and reflecting on each topic, you will gain a chance to develop the habit of a daily spiritual routine, an opportunity to increase your knowledge of truth from Scripture, and an occasion for God to engage and renew your mind and heart.

This journal was created and written by the TJ staff team (Kevin Applegate, Sue Nilson Kibbey, and Carolyn Slaughter) of Ginghamsburg Church in Tipp City, Ohio. The *Transformation Journal* cover and interior design is by Tracey Obenour.

COMPONENTS OF THIS JOURNAL

This *Transformation Journal* is arranged in weekly sections. Each week is designed to begin on Sunday and end on Saturday. They are not dated, however, so you can start at any time of the year. If you fall behind in your daily use of the TJ, just pick up with the next reading for that day of the week and resume your momentum.

Take a look at the first week and you'll see the following:

• A thought-provoking question that establishes the focus for each day;
• A "Focus Point" that follows up on the daily question, plus Scripture readings for each day;
• Journal/reflection questions to help you further unpack the meaning of the Scripture you've read and the implications for your faith;
• Space for personal study of each day's Scripture, allowing you to record your insights, thoughts, and prayers.

The best time to use this journal is when you are at your best! If you're a morning person, do your Bible reading and journaling/reflection time in the morning. If you're a night owl, do it at night. Invest time with God during the best part of your day, every day. The bottom line is that God deserves your best.

TIPS FOR USING YOUR *TRANSFORMATION JOURNAL*

1. Begin with prayer, asking God to open your heart and mind to new truths, to let you see today's Scripture through God's eyes, and to help you understand it with the heart and spirit of Jesus.
2. Carefully read the question, the Focus Point, and the Scriptures for the day.
3. Reread the Scripture passages, writing down any particular observations you make about what is happening, questions or ideas you have about what you are reading, and insights into what God might be doing or saying. Try to avoid isolating any single verse or using it as a "proof text" for something you believe. Instead observe God's bigger intentions of love and grace. What do you notice?
4. What did you learn from your observations that you can apply to how you live your life today? What bigger principles does God want you to understand? What spiritual truths from today's Scriptures challenge you to grow? What specific steps might God want you to take today in your attitude or your actions? Write them in your TJ.
5. Look at, ponder, and respond to the journal reflection questions that may take you even deeper into understanding the Scriptures you just read.
6. Close your time with God in prayer, asking God to show you how to apply what you've learned for life transformation. Write out your prayer in the TJ if you wish.

7. Meet with your cell group (small group) on a regular basis to discuss and interact together about the Scriptures you've read and what life applications you've made through the use of this *Transformation Journal*.

CELL GROUP GUIDE

Cell groups (small groups) are designed for investigating the Bible together as well as encouraging one another's spiritual growth, accountability, and relationship with Jesus. The following will help guide your cell group's meeting time as you use the *Transformation Journal* together.

Group Rules

1. A cell group practices confidentiality, which means what is shared in the group remains in the group.
2. A cell group is a safe place for people, where there is no judgment or ridicule for sharing thoughts, feelings, or past behaviors.
3. A cell group honors everyone's time by starting and ending the group on time.

Gather the People

Ask: "What was one God-moment you experienced this week?" and invite each person in the group to answer.

Bible Study

1. Choose and read as a group one or more of the primary Scriptures for the week.
2. Have each person share his or her response to one of this week's journal questions and the related Scripture passage.
3. Share personal stories about what God is currently transforming or changing in your life.

Caring Time

1. Ask each person to share prayer requests as well as blessings from the week.
2. Pray together as a group, acknowledging God's goodness and praying for the individual requests that were shared.
3. Pray that God brings others into your lives whom you may add to your cell group to increase your outreach.

the word on...
ITSELF (THE BIBLE)

sunday · *What Was God's Reason For Creating The Bible?*

_____

_____

_____

_____

_____

_____

_____

_____

_____

_____

_____

_____

_____

The Bible, known and accepted as the written word of God, is an important way God communicates with people in order to develop their relationship with God and to give life direction. Jesus demonstrated the importance of God's word by strategically quoting from the Old Testament throughout his earthly ministry.

Deuteronomy 8:1-11 and Matthew 4:1-11

• According to Deuteronomy 8, what did God promise God's people if they obeyed God's instructions (commands and laws) as written in the Scriptures?

• Think of a time when, as it did for Jesus in the wilderness, God's word came alive and made a strong difference as you faced a difficult situation or temptation. What happened?

The Holy Spirit actually comes to live within you when you open your life and heart to Jesus. The presence of the Spirit makes a personal relationship with God possible, and all of life begins to change, including your ability to grasp the meaning of God's written word and apply it to your daily living.

1 Corinthians 2:6-16 and Psalm 119:1-16

• According to 1 Corinthians 2, what effect does the Holy Spirit have in helping you understand spiritual truths from the Bible?

• From Psalm 119, list at least three transforming results that happen in your life as you internalize the Bible's message (here also called statutes, precepts, laws, and commands).

Most people want a life of meaning, fulfillment, and purpose—a life matching what God designed it to be. Yet your tendency may be to react to life experiences rather than to proactively seek the will of God. Every day, every follower of Christ needs to stop and think about where his or her life is headed, and that is best done in the revealing light of God's word—the Bible.

2 Timothy 3:10-17 and James 1:19-25

• What purpose does Bible study serve in the life of a believer (2 Timothy 3:16-17)?

• Just as you physically look into a mirror every morning before you face the world, James encourages you to do a daily spiritual check. As you look into the mirror of God's word, what needed adjustments to your life direction do you believe God is revealing to you?

wednesday

_____
_____
_____
_____
_____
_____
_____
_____
_____
_____
_____

The old saying "You only get as much out of something as you put into it" is especially applicable when it comes to Bible study. As a follower of Jesus, you can't expect your life to have maximum spiritual growth and impact in others' lives without your first immersing yourself in God's training manual, the Bible. In today's reading, the Israelites had disregarded their copy of the Scriptures many years before. But when God's word was redis-covered and its truths read, King Josiah went to work setting all things right according to what God desired.

2 Kings 22:1–23:25

• How did King Josiah respond personally to the new-found book of the Law, God's word? What actions did he take in response to hearing God's word for the first time?

• Is there anything in your life that needs to be "cleaned up" in order to line up with God's word, just as Josiah had to "clean up" his nation and the sinful activities they were practicing? If so, what?

thursday

_____
_____
_____
_____
_____
_____
_____
_____
_____
_____
_____

As you hear God speak through God's word about needed change in your life—and respond in obedience and surrender to the transforming power of the Holy Spirit—you will gradually begin to see yourself change, bit by bit, to take on the character and purpose of Jesus. Old habits will fade away, new habits reflecting God will take their place and a clearer picture of God's purpose for your life will begin to form.

Mark 4:1-20 and Deuteronomy 30:11-20

• Jesus understood the tendency to make excuses and rationalize disobedience. In Mark 4, what were the reasons preventing three of the seeds from producing a crop? What was the result of hearing and accepting (applying) the word, as symbolized by the fourth seed?

• In asking for full obedience as described in Deuteron-omy 30, is God asking you to do something impossible? Why or why not?

Paul, perhaps inspired by the Roman soldiers surrounding him during his imprisonment in Rome, used a sword to symbolize the word of God. Paul was very aware of the spiritual attack by forces of evil that comes against those who follow Jesus. The "sword of the Spirit" is the sharp instrument that helps you come against the enemy of evil, and it penetrates and judges your spirit as well.

Ephesians 6:10-18 and Hebrews 4:12-13

• Why do you think Paul chose to use the image of a sword when describing God's word, the Bible, to us?

• Read today's verses from Hebrews again. Think of a truth you have read in the Bible that has penetrated your heart and brought you new insight. What was it? How did it change your thinking and your actions?

Jesus validated the Scriptures as God-inspired and as God's means of communication with humanity. He presented the word of God as alive, transformational, and consisting of one central message—that Jesus was God's plan to reconnect and be in relationship with the people God loves. Jesus confronted the misuse of Scripture that reduced it to an intellectual exercise or a belief system made up of rules that judge and divide, rather than the living word of God that frees and transforms.

John 5:36-47 and 2 Timothy 2:15

• In John 5, Jesus was speaking to Jewish leaders. How were they misunderstanding and thereby misusing the Old Testament Scriptures?

• The "word of truth" in 2 Timothy is a reference to the Bible, God's word. If this verse describes God's expectation of you, what steps can you take to help yourself become better and better at being a "workman" as described?

the word on...
PRAYER

sunday
What Advice Did Jesus Give About How To Pray?

_____
_____
_____
_____
_____
_____
_____
_____
_____
_____
_____
_____
_____
_____
_____

Prayer was an integral part of Jesus' life, and the twelve men who surrounded him during his three years of ministry were privileged to have Jesus as a model in this area. This intimate connection with the Father, which gave Jesus power to accomplish God's mission, remained a mystery to them until they finally said to Jesus, "Teach us to pray."

Luke 11:1-11 and Matthew 6:5-15

• Matthew and Luke each gave their own unique perspective on Jesus' instructions on prayer, with certain things standing out in importance to each one. What did each one report?

• Which of their instructions are most helpful to improving your daily prayer life?

God's word teaches that perseverance in prayer yields amazing results. Rather than a grocery list of requests submitted for God's approval, prayer becomes an on-going conversation with God about God's will for you, the well-being of others, and the fulfillment of God's purpose on Earth. Even back in Old Testament times, Abraham's persevering prayers yielded miraculous results.

Luke 18:1-8 and Genesis 18:16-33

• What in today's Scriptures would encourage a follower of Christ to persevere long term in prayer?

• For what or whom have you let go of praying and need to resume?

When I Pray, What Is My Ultimate Goal? **tuesday**

True prayer ultimately brings a close connection with God, through which you submit your mind, heart, and will to God for alignment with God's heart and will. This truly is the most important purpose of prayer (not just asking for protection and blessings!). The night before his crucifixion, Jesus prayed for his followers' alignment with God's will and heart, and then began the journey to the cross with his own time of painfully surrendering himself to God's will and greater purpose.

John 17:1-26 and Matthew 26:36-46

• From John 17, list at least three "alignment" requests Jesus makes to God on behalf of his followers. What request does he make for himself in Matthew 26?

• Some call Jesus' prayer for God's will to be done, not his own (Matthew 26:42), "the prayer that never fails." Why do you think this is—and do you agree?

wednesday
What Is The Value Of Praying With Other Believers?

_____

_____

_____

_____

_____

_____

_____

_____

_____

_____

_____

_____

Following the resurrection and ascension of Jesus, his followers gathered together and formed communities that shared all things in common, especially prayer. They continued to grow in their understanding of God's plan and their trust in God to handle all things. Their experiences give followers of Jesus today the assurance that miracles can happen when believers pray together.

Matthew 18:18-20 and Acts 12:1-19

• In Matthew 18, Jesus taught that group accountability in prayer brings miraculous results. What did he say is the supernatural component when believers gather together to pray?

• The people in Acts 12 prayed together for Peter's situation—and God responded with a miracle that surprised them. Have you ever been surprised by a miraculous answer to prayer? How did you and others react?

thursday
What Difference Does Praying Before Making A Decision Really Make?

_____

_____

_____

_____

_____

_____

_____

_____

_____

_____

_____

_____

Within just a few chapters of Scripture (Luke 5–9), four different occasions are described in which Jesus sought God in prayer, either alone or in the company of his disciples. It is clear that going to God in prayer was a regular pattern in Jesus' life and always happened before major decisions, significant ministry, and the working of miracles.

Luke 5:12-16, 6:12-19, and 9:18-36

• In each of today's readings, what God-empowered event happened in conjunction with Jesus' spending time in prayer?

• What decision or life situation are you facing that needs intentional time in prayer with God? After reading today's Scriptures, what result can you expect?

The Bible clearly teaches that your state of heart and mind have everything to do with your prayer life. It is only when you have asked forgiveness for your wrongs and have brought yourself sincerely and wholly before God that your prayers can become aligned with God's best intentions and miraculous power. Although you do not need certain words or posture for effective prayer, examining your intent and preparing the state of your heart for prayer are vitally important.

Mark 11:12-24 and James 4:2-10

• According to today's Scriptures, what is necessary in order to pray effectively? What can make your prayer life ineffective?

• Which of these most challenge you in your prayer life?

The Old Testament contains a story of a king whose pride prevented him from praying or even paying attention to God. After God's servant Daniel interpreted the king's dream, God allowed painful life experiences to happen that eventually drove the king into true prayer. Without a healthy relationship with God through prayer, your personal welfare and future are at stake.

Daniel 4:19-37 and 2 Chronicles 7:14

• When King Nebuchadnezzar's focus changed to prayer (Daniel 4:34-37), his life changed. How?

• Daniel's advice to King Nebuchadnezzar in 4:27 reflects the priorities of a humble servant of God. How does this advice offer guidance for your prayer life?

the word on...
COMMUNITY

sunday
What Is It That Seems To Draw Me Into Christian Community?

If you are like most people, you have an innate desire to be with other people. This desire comes directly from God, because God created you for relationship. As a Christian, however, an even more specific calling is on your life for community. As a follower of Jesus, you have been inducted into a powerful community of believers that has God as its center and sharing the love of Jesus Christ as its mission.

1 John 1:1-10 and
1 Corinthians 1:1-9

• What are the benefits of belonging to God's "fellowship of believers"? What do those who are called into God's community share in common?

• According to today's readings, around what has God drawn us together as Christians?

The earliest group of Christian believers probably asked this question too, but they quickly decided what was important for them as a group. A first priority was the need to be in close Christian community in order to be encouraged and inspired to do the mission to which Jesus had called them. The spiritual growth and support they experienced in Christian community allowed them to begin the incredible task of making disciples of the whole world.

Acts 2:29-47

• What made this community of believers so committed to one another? How did they show it?

• If you totally devoted yourself daily to a Christian community that included biblical teaching, deep fellowship, and prayer, how would your spiritual life grow? Which of these is lacking right now for you?

What is it about being in Christian fellowship that makes you stronger in your faith? There is definitely strength in numbers, and the Christian life is no different. It would be to your peril to think you can be just as strong and grow just as much in your spiritual life without the help and encouragement of your Christian brothers and sisters.

Hebrews 10:19-25, 3:12-13, and Galatians 6:1-2

• List the five "let us" statements, or callings on the community, from Hebrews 10:22-25. Why do you think it is easier to worship or have hope in Christ in a community of people rather than by yourself?

• Describe a time when you were encouraged or spurred on by another Christian brother or sister. Have you ever encouraged another believer? What happened?

wednesday

_____
_____
_____
_____
_____
_____
_____
_____
_____
_____
_____

Being in Christian community is a crucial priority—since most, if not all of us, are influenced by the world around us. That is just our nature. Just as many people begin speaking in the accent of the people around them after a period of time, you too will take on the flavor of those you spend the most time with on a regular basis.

Proverbs 13:20
and 2 Corinthians 6:14–7:1

• How does the image of being yoked together give you insight about those with whom you can and can't have a close relationship?

• What will it take for you to influence non-Christians with your life and yet not be negatively influenced by them?

thursday

_____
_____
_____
_____
_____
_____
_____
_____
_____
_____
_____

If there were one clear message about being in Christian community together, it would be the call to love. The whole world should be able to look into every group of Christians and see the overwhelming presence of love and commitment to one another. God's word clearly describes the importance of every single person called into Christian community, even if each one is very different from the others. God has reasons for you to value those in community with you who are nothing like yourself.

1 Corinthians 12:12-27
and 1 John 4:7-21

• According to 1 Corinthians 12, what is the purpose for the diversity of people found within Christian community? Why do we need one another?

• Is it possible to truly love God and hate others with whom you are in community? Why or why not?

God has definitely called us to be in community for our protection and strength, but it doesn't stop there. God desires that all of creation be in right relationship with God, and we are the hands and feet to bring that about. One important aspect of Christian fellowship is our partnership in the mission of Christ. Just as we partner with other believers in living out our lives, we also partner with God in the mighty work of redeeming the world by bringing the love of Jesus to all people.

Philippians 1:3-11 and 2:1-4

• What does the word *partnership* mean to you? Define the word. What kind of partnerships do you share with other Christians you're around regularly?

• If we are equal partners with God in redeeming the world, what is God's part and what is ours?

One of the awesome aspects about being in Christian community is God's miraculous power that works within us. In calling us to partnership in building God's kingdom, God imparts mighty power in and through us as Christ's "body" to accomplish the extraordinary. In fact, you can't even imagine all that God has in store for us together!

Ephesians 3:14–4:6
and Acts 4:31-35

• Which by-product of God's love (as described in the Ephesians passages) encourages you the most?

• In Acts 4:31, a direct connection between speaking the word of God boldly and being filled with the Holy Spirit is shown. How did this affect the early Christian community? How could it affect your community today?

the word on...
SERVING

_____
_____
_____
_____
_____
_____
_____
_____
_____
_____
_____
_____
_____

Throughout his earthly ministry, Jesus turned the common religious understanding of his day upside down. And in his last few hours on Earth, he cemented the idea of serving in the hearts and minds of his followers with a dramatic example. Through a graphic demonstration of caring for others, Jesus provided a powerful overall message about serving.

John 13:1-17

• Do you think Jesus was telling his followers to physically wash the feet of others? What else could he have meant?

• Who is the person who could use a cleansing, refreshing touch of care from you today?

While Jesus was on Earth he represented God's words, character, and work. Among Jesus' last instructions to his followers was the challenge to continue this work. Jesus also promised to empower his followers for serving beyond what even Jesus himself did, according to what you ask.

John 14:1-14

• What promises did Jesus give his followers in today's reading?

• Write a prayer naming which promise you need most today, and claim it with confidence!

Jesus got a variety of responses to his invitation to follow him. Not everyone liked or accepted the cost involved in total commitment, yet Jesus commissioned seventy-two who were willing to be totally involved in his work of harvesting, healing, and spreading the gospel. The results of their serving were miraculous.

Luke 9:51–10:20

• How did Jesus respond to the excuses offered in Luke 9:57-62? To the rejection found in Luke 10:8-16?

• What excuse do you need to eliminate when it comes to serving others?

wednesday

_____
_____
_____
_____
_____
_____
_____
_____
_____
_____
_____
_____

The Holy Spirit gives supernatural abilities (spiritual gifts) to every follower of Jesus to do ministry. Each follower is uniquely gifted by God and is equally valuable in God's service. If God has equipped you for ministry, God will hold you accountable for managing your gifts wisely and using them cheerfully for God's purpose.

Romans 12:1-8
and 2 Timothy 2:20-26

• What do today's Scriptures say about how to prepare yourself for God's use in serving?

• According to the Timothy reading, what attitudes are the ones that please God as you serve?

thursday

_____
_____
_____
_____
_____
_____
_____
_____
_____
_____
_____
_____

Even Jesus' closest companions didn't understand the selflessness required to complete Jesus' mission. True service is not about the benefits you receive or positioning yourself for greater power and influence. True service is about emptying yourself for others.

Matthew 20:20-28
and Philippians 2:3-11

• What lesson(s) from Jesus' response to the other ten disciples (Matthew 20:24-28) did James and John need to learn?

• In what particular situation do you need to choose humility and service over the desire to have power and control?

When you name Jesus as Lord (absolute authority, Master), you acknowledge yourself as his servant. A servant's role is to obey the master; complete obedience is nothing out of the ordinary for a servant. Servants of Jesus do what the Master asks without complaint, and serve others as if serving him.

Luke 17:7-10
and Colossians 3:18—4:1

• Describe the mind-set for godly serving represented in these Scriptures. What challenges you?

• How could things be different today if you treated others the way you would treat Jesus?

In a world where the message of Jesus can be unpopular and divisive, Jesus' followers can expect conflict, even within their own families. Yet serving the least and the lost will bring Christ's followers great reward.

Matthew 5:38-41 and 10:32-42

• What do Jesus' followers (then and now) face as a result of serving him?

• Has your family been divided or united because of Jesus? Would your willingness to "go the second mile" to serve them help create unity?

the word on...
STEWARDSHIP

sunday

What Does It Mean To Practice "Stewardship"?

Stewardship is the management of and accountability for something that belongs to someone else, especially the human management of God's resources. When Jesus left Earth, he entrusted us all with his mission and the resources to fulfill it. Your choices of what to do here and now must be done in light of Jesus' return and your accountability to God.

Luke 12:35-48

• What characterizes a good and faithful manager of God's resources (12:42-45)? What will be the good manager's reward?

• List those things you believe God has entrusted you personally to manage on God's behalf. How seriously are you taking these responsibilities?

Integrity is a cornerstone of stewardship. One who is trustworthy and competent is promoted in the business world; those who have proved to be trustworthy in the spiritual arena are also given greater responsibility.

Luke 16:1-15

• In Matthew 16:13 Jesus named the tension between loving God and loving money. From verse 15, what is the outcome of loving money? Of loving God?

• Honoring God with your money and possessions demonstrates that you value true spiritual wealth. In what use of your money could you give God greater honor?

What Am I Supposed To Do With God's Resources? **tuesday**

Jesus recognized that God's resources would be entrusted to a variety of people, representing different levels of commitment and willingness to follow through with their God-honoring use. Using your gifts, talents, financial resources, and time appropriately may be costly, but in the end it costs much more to choose not to obey.

Luke 19:1-27

• The third servant (verses 20-21) operated under a faulty perception of the master. How did that influence his actions and reward?

• In what way do you think your perception of God is influencing your investment of the talents and resources Jesus has given you? Which servant are you most like?

wednesday

_____
_____
_____
_____
_____
_____
_____
_____
_____
_____
_____
_____

Paul's example in 1 Corinthians 9 shows an approach to serving that was joyful and purposeful. He was not motivated by monetary rewards but rather was willing to do whatever it took "to win as many as possible" to Christ.

1 Corinthians 9:7-27

• What rights did Paul have as an apostle (spiritual leader)? Why did he give them up?

• What would you be willing to give up financially, relationally, or professionally in order that you "might win some"?

thursday

_____
_____
_____
_____
_____
_____
_____
_____
_____
_____
_____

You are to grow in maturity in Christ and are provided the resources personally and through the church to become a mature follower of Jesus. It's up to you to manage those resources by making the hard choices that will accomplish the goal.

Ephesians 4:11–5:20

• You are to "be careful then how you live, not as unwise people but as wise." From today's Scripture, what are some behaviors that characterize wise living?

• As you grow in maturity in Christ, what are some old patterns that are fading away? What new patterns are replacing them?

Psalm 90 recalls a prayer of Moses as he prepared God's people to enter the Promised Land. An example of a life well lived, Moses knew the importance of maximizing the time granted us to accomplish God's purpose and fully serve God.

Psalm 90

• List the references to time in this psalm. What insight do you have as to what it means to rightly number your days?

• How are you doing in managing your time in a way that honors and serves God? What could be improved?

Your ability to manage God's resources well lies in your ability to embrace simplicity as a life discipline. Living with just one focus simplifies you on the inside and results in freedom from attachment to things, schedules, and the need for status, position, and success. Your focus is redirected to Christ alone.

Matthew 6:19-34 and 11:25-30

• Simplicity is an active pursuit, not a passive lifestyle. What one thing are you to pursue that will clarify your focus and simplify your life (Matthew 6:33)?

• One of the fruits of a simple lifestyle is greater freedom from worry and anxiety. What causes you the most worry? How could simplifying your life reduce the worry?

the word on...
LOVE VERSUS LUST

sunday
What Is The Difference Between Godly Love And Worldly Lust?

Because godly love acted out through your life is such a powerful force for good, the power of evil has fabricated a very strong and destructive counterfeit: lust. Just as godly love represents giving, sacrificing, and looking out for others, lust acts out in self-seeking, self-benefiting behaviors that ultimately harm others and destroy relationships. Because lust is such a strong force, you must continually stay alert to its temptation and stay faithful to living out God's love in your behavior instead.

1 Thessalonians 4:3-9, 1 Peter 4:1-8, and Ephesians 5:1-7

• From today's passages, how is passionate lust different from godly love? How can acting on lust take advantage of and wrong other people?

• Think through your relationships as well as your work, priorities, and goals. Are your choices in each of them based on godly love, or on self-benefiting lust?

At times it's difficult to get an accurate picture of love. Popular culture continually bombards everyone with the emotional aspect of love but rarely describes the active sacrifice that real love requires. True godly love is not just based on feelings but expresses itself as an active commitment to others—always wanting the best for them, instead of thinking first of yourself.

1 Corinthians 13:1-13

• In 1 Corinthians 13, what active characteristics of love are named? What does real love not do?

• Think about each characteristic of love and write down the names of persons who have loved you in this way. Give thanks for each person.

Because authentic love is so sacrificial, you may have a hard time honestly loving other persons in your own power. In fact, without God's help you could never truly love or even understand love. God is the essence of love. With God present in your heart, you can truly love others by an outpouring of God's love through you.

1 John 4:7-21 and John 13:34-35

• According to today's readings, what is the most visible sign of God's love? How does loving others prove that you know God?

• To whom can you specifically show God's love today?

wednesday
What Is Loving Others Supposed To Look Like?

You have read about the true characteristics of love and the source of that love, but how does that love actually affect your relationship with others? Godly love puts others first, just as Christ himself loved you enough to die for you. The Bible is clear: love is an action word.

1 John 3:11-24 and John 15:12-13

• What particular actions of love are named in the 1 John passage?

• "Laying down your life" for others means choosing unselfish actions on behalf of others. Give an example of someone whose actions fit that definition. What did the person do?

thursday
How Can I Know God Genuinely Loves Me?

Mere human words could never fully describe the incredibly deep love that God has for you. As you read today's passages, be encouraged that God's love for you is higher, deeper, and wider than you could ever imagine or comprehend. Because God has first loved you, you are empowered to love others in a healthy way.

Romans 8:31-39, 5:6-8, and John 3:16-17

• How much does God love you? To what extent has God been willing to go in order to show you that love?

• How does God's unmatched love for you motivate you to love others? What things in your life do you need God's love to conquer?

It is easier to talk about demonstrating God's extravagant love than to really get down to active caring for others. The Bible story today shows a great example of extraordinary love—a love willing to do whatever it takes, a willingness to pour out one's life to care for another's needs. You show your love for Jesus by serving selflessly through loving actions.

Luke 7:36-50

• Why did Jesus appreciate the woman more than his dinner host, the Pharisee named Simon?

• When have you loved someone with actions rather than words? Write down an action of love you can take today.

Many Scripture passages urge believers to love one another. The strongest witness that Christians bring to the rest of the world is the example of modeling godly community bonded together through love. Encouraging, serving, honoring, and lifting one another up are all part of what God desires.

Romans 13:8-10, 12:9-13, and Galatians 5:13-14

• From the Scripture readings, list the "nonnegotiables" given about how Christians are to demonstrate love for one another.

• Write your own definition of what it means to "love your neighbor as yourself." Is God challenging you in any specific way to better live this out?

the word on...
HOSPITALITY

sunday *What Does Hospitality Look Like To God?*

You might generally think of "hospitality" as an industry (hotels and restaurants) or as entertaining (throwing a great party). In the Bible the word *hospitality* means showing love to strangers. When you extend hospitality, you generously receive people not only into your home and circle of friends but into your life.

Matthew 25:31-46
and 1 Peter 4:7-11

• For what seven actions in Matthew 25:35-36 will Jesus hold his followers accountable?

• Of these seven actions toward others, which do you need to start practicing more?

Hospitality is about extending God's grace and inviting people to experience the love of Jesus. Being willing to humble yourself and sacrificially be involved with all people is a critical part of hospitality. Even when people excuse themselves as too busy or too involved, keep on asking and welcoming until God's house is filled.

Luke 14:1-24

• What do you learn about the difference between society's values and Jesus' values from today's verses?

• In what ways have you been subtly influenced by society's values rather than Jesus' values?

"In reception of the poor and of pilgrims the greatest care and solicitude should be shown, because it is especially in them that Christ is received" (Saint Benedict, A.D. 480–543). The greatest benefit of all is experiencing Jesus through those whom you welcome into your life.

Luke 24:13-36 and Hebrews 13:1-3

• In the story in Luke 24, why did the two men not recognize Jesus? What opened their eyes to him?

• In what current situation or relationship do you most need your eyes opened to see Jesus?

The key to hospitality is love—not as an emotion but as assertive, practical actions that reach out to care for others. Your willingness to apply the New Testament's teachings on demonstrating this kind of practical love will determine the climate of your family, your local church, and your community.

Romans 12:9-21, Acts 2:42-47, and 3 John 1:1-14

• What makes you think the individuals within the Acts 2 believers' community were practicing what Paul taught in Romans 12:9-21?

• Based on Romans 12, what loving action could you take this week toward someone who is difficult to love?

As the people in Philippi responded to the gospel message through Paul, they opened their hearts and homes to him and his traveling companions. Entire households were changed. When the gospel enters a home through just one believer, a chain reaction begins that influences not only a family but also future generations.

Acts 16:11-40

• Paul and Silas were falsely accused, severely beaten, and thrown into a dark, damp cell with other prisoners. Why did they trust the jailer to take them to his home? What was the result?

• When have you stepped out in faith and trusted another person's offer of hospitality? What happened?

Paul was one of the most well-traveled apostles, completing three missionary journeys around the Mediterranean area. Roman inns of the time were known as dangerous, dirty, and flea infested, so traveling teachers, including Paul, depended on the local communities of believers for hospitality instead.

Acts 21:1-16 and 28:1-10

• In how many homes did Paul stay, as described by these verses? What acts of "unusual kindness" were done for Paul?

• Is it difficult for you to accept or receive help from others? Why or why not?

Hospitality is bigger than opening your home; it has to do with opening your heart. The love you received from Jesus flows out from you, and this enables you to welcome others as Jesus does. You may not like what you see or hear; your comfort zone may be pushed to the max. But the directive is clear—we all are to welcome the stranger.

James 2:14-26 and 1 John 3:16-24

• According to today's Scriptures, how does faith go beyond lip service to action?

• John's definition of love is found in 1 John 3:16-18. Rewrite it in your own words. How does it differ from the world's "definition" of love?

the word on...
SELF-DISCIPLINE

sunday
What Do My Christian Faith And Self-Discipline Have To Do With Each Other?

Even though you are saved from your sin through the free gift of grace from Jesus Christ, you are called to take active steps in learning to live a self-controlled life. Although difficult at times, the call to disciplined living helps you learn victory over your old sinful nature that continues to war against you and your relationship with God. Just like an accomplished athlete or skilled musician, you, too, must train daily if you wish to become the person God desires you to be.

1 Thessalonians 5:4-11 and 1 Corinthians 9:24-27

• What kind of behavior represents people of the light or day, versus people of darkness or night?

• Have you ever trained for something? Relate that experience with training yourself to run the Christian race. What must you do to succeed?

Before you were a Christian you were powerless against your sinful desires. However, because you have received new life in Christ Jesus, you can succeed in defeating those desires! Since Christ now reigns in your heart, sin no longer will rule you as long as you commit daily to live in God's will and power, not your own.

Romans 6:1-18 and 13:12-14

• Romans 6 refers to slavery and freedom. What are the characteristics of each?

• List several ways that God can use you to be an "instrument of righteousness" this week.

Jesus not only came to save you from your sinful self but also sent the Holy Spirit to give you the power to overcome ongoing temptations. Without the Holy Spirit's help, you could never rise above those powerful pulls of selfishness and pride. But through the Spirit, you can gain the victory and radiate the characteristics of God such as love and joy.

2 Timothy 1:7
and Galatians 5:1, 13-26

• List the differences between the acts of the sinful nature and the fruit of the Spirit.

• The Holy Spirit brings into your life power, love, and self-control. Which of these characteristics needs to be revealed through your life more?

wednesday

_____

_____

_____

_____

_____

_____

_____

_____

_____

_____

_____

_____

All through history God has called God's people to a disciplined, obedient life of faith. Even when catastrophe strikes, God is close to those who have trained themselves to honor God in all ways. Disobedient behavior separates you from God's companionship, but a disciplined walk of faith deepens your relationship with God.

Titus 2:11-14 and Psalm 34:1-22

• Psalm 34:12-14 describes characteristics of a self-disciplined lifestyle that honors God. According to this psalm, how does God bless those who practice them?

• According to Titus, what is God's goal for you as a self-controlled, godly person?

thursday

_____

_____

_____

_____

_____

_____

_____

_____

_____

_____

_____

_____

According to the Scriptures, every day you are called to set not only your mind but also your heart on "things above"—all that represents God's best for you and for God's world. Paul's letter to the Colossians is specific in its description of what it means to take off your "old self" and put on the new. When you practice this discipline daily, you actually allow God to bring God's love, joy, and peace through your life to others.

Colossians 3:1-17

• Make a list of the "old life" practices versus "new life" actions listed in this passage. Which ones do you still struggle to take off? Put on?

• How can you better keep your mind and heart focused on God?

Trusting in God's design for life produces motivation for spiritual growth. Daniel and his friends kept God's priorities even while in captivity, and God blessed their commitment to personal training and discipline. Their lives have become a testimony even to believers today as a result of their self-disciplined, faith-filled choices.

Daniel 1:1-21 and Matthew 6:33

• List the different ways God blessed Daniel's faithfulness and self-discipline. What hard choices did Daniel have to make?

• What are the top priorities in your Christian life? What self-disciplined choices might you need to make to keep them true priorities?

The Scriptures are clear: the best way to avoid the negative influence of those who pull you away from following Christ is to steer clear of their company. Friends who struggle to stay obedient to their own faith may also drag you down. Instead, connect yourself with other self-disciplined believers who will encourage you to stay the course.

Psalm 1:1-6

• What does Psalm 1 identify as the result of staying focused and self-disciplined toward God's word?

• What "fruit" has your practice of self-discipline yielded so far?

the word on...
TESTING

sunday
What Is God Trying To Accomplish Through "Testing" Times In My Life?

_____

_____

_____

_____

_____

_____

_____

_____

_____

_____

_____

_____

When life is comfortable and convenient, you may not have a sense of need for God. But when the blessings of God are taken away, the true character of a person comes to light. Job (a man of God described in the Old Testament) as well as first-century Jesus followers described in the New Testament provide examples of what happens in seasons of testing—and what the results can be.

1 Peter 1:3-12 and Job 23:1-12

• What hope do you find in 1 Peter 1:7 about God's desired outcome as a result of trials you face?

• Like Job, during times of testing you may feel distant from God. According to Job 23:1-12, what helped Job stay faithful and confident? How can these same things help you in times of testing?

Abraham, a follower of God, faced every extreme test and trial placed before him with the kind of faith that kept his eyes on God and God's trustworthiness. Even with the life of his child at stake, Abraham's faith was not blind and unreasoned; it was based in Abraham's confidence in the character of God and God's good intentions toward him.

Hebrews 11:8-19
and Genesis 22:1-19

• According to Hebrews 11, in what three ways did God "test" Abraham? In what way did God provide for Abraham in Genesis 22?

• Think of a time when, like Abraham, your faith has been tested. How did God provide?

It seems like it would have been easy for the Israelites to trust God, given their miraculous release out of Egypt and God's provision for them in the desert. Instead they followed the human tendency to take God's blessings for granted, demonstrate ingratitude, and even grumble against God. God's purpose in allowing them challenges and trials was to humble them and help them learn to trust.

Exodus 15:22–16:35

• Choose five words from this passage that you think describe the relationship between the Israelites and God. Why did you choose those words?

• What five words would describe your relationship with God? Is God working to humble you and teach you greater trust, as God did with the Israelites?

wednesday
Does God Use Other People To "Test" Me At Times?

After the conquest of the Promised Land under Joshua and following his death, the Israelites began a disappointing cyclical pattern of sin, judgment, and repentance, which they repeated many times. God finally allowed the Israelites to face "testing" of their faith through attacks by enemy nations. God's desire is always to see a response of faith and obedience.

Judges 2:6–3:6

• As described in Judges 2:20–3:4, how did God allow the people of Israel to be "tested"? What results did God hope to see?

• Can you identify a time when God tested you like God tested the Israelites? Who did God use, and how are you different as a result?

thursday
In What Other Ways Does God Sometimes "Test" Me?

God may test you by prompting you to ask difficult and challenging questions about your priorities. As you come to grips with what God's priorities really are, you have the opportunity to remove what may be blocking you from a vital relationship with God. What feels impossible to overcome is possible with God!

Luke 18:18-30

• Why did Jesus ask the rich young ruler to sell all his possessions? Why do you think Jesus' request was a "test" for the ruler?

• What challenging question of priorities has God used to "test" your faithfulness? How did the question present itself?

You may feel like God is testing you by being slow to act in a given situation. But it may actually be God's means of revealing Jesus in a great way (John 11:4). For example, Jesus dearly loved his friends Mary, Martha, and Lazarus, yet was purposely slow in responding to them. The depth of Jesus' love for them was not in question; Jesus used his timing in a difficult situation so others would come to know him.

John 11:1-45

• What were the different responses of Mary and Martha when Jesus finally arrived?

• For what answer from Jesus are you currently waiting? What does today's Scripture teach you about the importance of staying faithful in times of waiting on God?

After times of trial, testing, questioning, and suffering, God restores. Recognition of God's activity in your life may come slowly. God's outcome for you may be different than you expected. Just like silver is refined in the process of making fine jewelry, God refines your character, renews your faith, and enables you to see the abundance of great things God is doing and creating in your life.

Psalm 66

• What "tests" had the psalmist endured? What blessings from God does the psalmist name?

• Make a list of the blessings from God you have received, and write a prayer thanking God for providing so abundantly.

the word on...
CHARACTER

What Do The Choices I Make Toward Achieving Goals Say About My Character?

_____

_____

_____

_____

_____

_____

_____

_____

_____

_____

_____

Before Jacob and his twin brother Esau were born, God revealed to Rebekah something out of the ordinary: contrary to law and custom, her younger son Jacob would become God's appointed leader rather than his older brother (Genesis 25:23). Through Rebekah's actions to "help" God bring this about, Jacob received his blessing, but created years of animosity, anger, and pain within the family.

Genesis 27:1–28:9

• What character flaws do you see in each of the individuals in today's verses? What loss did each experience as a result of Jacob and Rebekah's deception?

• In what circumstance right now are you tempted to "help God out" rather than wait for God's timing?

The transformation of your character is a gradual process and begins through your willingness to honestly encounter God. Regardless of Jacob's character flaws and weaknesses, God showed up for him. Like Jacob, as you grow in your relationship with God, your character will be challenged and developed through staying faithful, whatever your circumstances.

Genesis 28:10–29:30

• What was God's promise to Jacob (28:15)? How did Jacob show good character despite being tricked by Laban?

• When was someone close to you dishonest and deceptive? What did you do? How could you have shown better godly character in responding to his or her dishonesty?

The values and outlook with which you approach life will influence not only you but also everyone around you. In today's reading, Rachel and Leah demonstrated the jealous, competitive, and manipulative behavior that can result when one seeks purpose in life through another person, role, or function rather than through God. When your character is not godly, your focus will shift to the wrong priorities.

Genesis 29:31–30:43

• Whom did Rachel and Leah's race to have children affect? What competition arose between Jacob and Laban? What was the outcome of each of these situations?

• Think about the priorities, values, and outlook you demonstrate at home, at work, or in your community. Will these expressions of your character most likely create blessing or pain in the future?

wednesday

_____

Although far from totally transformed in character himself, Jacob finally had his fill of his father-in-law's selfishness. Under God's direction, and with the support and cooperation of his wives, Jacob headed home to Canaan. In some situations, a clean break is necessary to protect future generations from negative patterns, but listening and following God's direction to make positive steps toward change is right in every situation.

Genesis 31:1-55

• What examples of the family pattern of dishonesty and deception can you identify in today's verses?

• Every family has negative patterns that need to change and be aligned with God's will and purpose. What patterns in your family need to be adjusted or broken? What positive first step could you take?

thursday

_____

After twenty years of remembering Esau's hatred, Jacob felt guilt and terror as he finally faced his wronged brother. After making his own plans to meet Esau, Jacob encountered God in a whole new way that left him with a physical reminder of God's power and provision. The wounds you carry from broken relationships and failures become powerful reminders of your inability to do life on your own and your need for God's transformational power. Only God can make the difference in you and in the lives of those you have wronged.

Genesis 32:1–33:20

• What changes in character appear to have taken place in Jacob? In Esau?

• Over what have you wrestled with God? What was the outcome?

Like Jacob, you are a work in progress. Perfection is not equivalent to being flawless. It is an indicator of your consistent growth in character and maturity, increasingly reflecting Christ's values through obedience. As you mature spiritually, so will your attitudes, behavior, and capacity to love as God loves.

Matthew 5:38-48 and Psalm 15:1-5

• What do today's verses say about what God wants from and for you as you live out your spiritual relationship through Jesus?

• Which of the instructions in today's verses is most challenging for you to follow?

Character development comes through the series of trials and challenges God allows in your life. In every difficult situation the Holy Spirit is available to strengthen your responses and to intercede for God's perfect result to come about in your life—your transformation into the image (character) of Christ.

Romans 8:9-30

• According to Romans, what role does the Spirit play in your character transformation? What does it look like to be led by the Spirit?

• In what area do you believe God is challenging you to grow further in your character development?

the word on...
PERSEVERANCE

sunday

Why Does God Let Me Experience Trouble And Challenges?

_____

_____

_____

_____

_____

_____

_____

_____

_____

_____

_____

_____

_____

Most days, life is sprinkled with challenges—some large, some small. You can "count it all joy" because God's purpose is not to shake your faith or pull you down spiritually. God is about building you up and strengthening you! Learn to look beyond your present circumstances to see what God is producing in and through you: perseverance.

James 1:2-12 and John 15:1-11

• According to James 1, what can you expect to happen as a result of your commitment to persevere in the midst of challenges?

• From John 15, what is the relationship between your connection with Christ and your ability to persevere and be productive for God?

Moses and the Israelites finally fled slavery in Egypt to head for God's Promised Land, but their journey required both perseverance and faith. When Pharaoh, ruler of Egypt, realized they were gone, he sent his best army to pursue them. Moses' faith in God led the Israelites to persevere even amid their fear—and a miracle unfolded.

Exodus 14:5-31

• What was Moses' response to the Israelites' terror? How did they step out in faith?

• When you persevere in faith, God makes a way before you. Name a time when God has opened a path as you persevered.

It's easy in the face of conflict, hardship, persecution, and suffering to feel sorry for yourself, become fearful, or just shut down in your emotions, relationships, and area of service. Moses became frustrated with the complaints of the Israelite people. Paul and James, no strangers to hardship and persecution, gave wise counsel on how to persevere in challenging times.

Exodus 17:1-7, James 5:7-11, and Galatians 6:7-10

• What did Moses do when the grumbling of the Israelites became too much to bear? What did God provide to help him persevere?

• List at least three attitudes or actions from James and Galatians that you could adopt today that would make a difference in your ability to persevere.

wednesday *How Do God's Grace And Perseverance Go Together?*

_____

_____

_____

_____

_____

_____

_____

_____

_____

_____

_____

_____

By God's grace (God's unconditional love, acceptance, and provision) in Jesus, not only have you been forgiven, but also you are connected to God in a very personal way. That connection means God's grace continues to flow in your life regardless of your life situation, providing everything you need to persevere and be all God has in mind for you.

Romans 5:1-5, 2 Peter 1:3-11, and Psalm 20

• Paul wrote to the Romans that perseverance ultimately leads to hope. How?

• Seven qualities are listed in 2 Peter 1 that we are urged to develop. Which do you already see in your life? Which need some work?

thursday *How Can Other Believers Help Encourage Me To Persevere?*

_____

_____

_____

_____

_____

_____

_____

_____

_____

_____

_____

Moses had a major leadership role with God's people and a long journey on which to lead them. Though some of the people were complainers and grumblers, God also raised up faithful friends who helped Moses keep his perspective. Even in a crisis, God used Moses' friends to help Moses persevere to victory.

Exodus 17:8-16 and Psalm 138

• What assistance did Moses' friends provide? What reward came from their perseverance?

• Like the writer of Psalm 138, of what great provisions of God can you remind yourself every day to help you keep persevering? Make a list.

Just as world events came together preceding Jesus' first entry into time and space as a human being (Galatians 4:4), so world events will come together in preparation for Jesus' return to Earth. How Jesus' followers handle themselves as they anticipate his coming has impact for them and for the advancement of his kingdom.

Matthew 24:1-14, 42-51, and 25:1-13

• What does Jesus promise those who persevere till the end?

• If Jesus returned today, would he be pleased with your choices and level of perseverance?

Jesus told his followers that they would experience persecution and trouble because of their connection with him (John 16:33). Today's Scriptures assure you of God's unconditional and eternal commitment to you as a follower of Jesus—and God's ultimate victory.

Romans 8:28-40 and Isaiah 40:25-31

• Over what threats are we more than conquerors (Romans 8:35-40)?

• Of those you listed, which are most real to you now? Write a prayer thanking God for defeating those threats through Christ and claiming God's power to walk in victory over them.

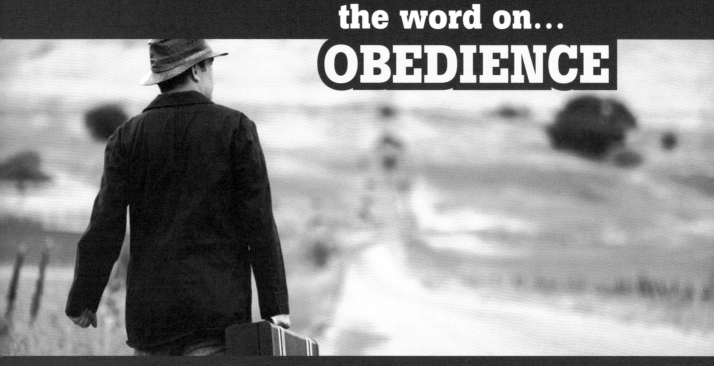

the word on...
OBEDIENCE

sunday — *What Is My First Step In Becoming An Obedient Child Of God?*

The first step in consistently obeying God is honestly knowing and understanding how God wants you to live—and saying yes. Jonah knew what God wanted him to do but disobeyed, with disastrous consequences that jeopardized himself as well as those around him. The results of his disobedience nearly brought Jonah to his death.

Jonah 1:1–2:10

• What did God want Jonah to do? Why do you think he disobeyed?

• In Jonah 2:9, Jonah finally agreed to obey God. How far on a path of disobedience have you ever gone before you finally turned back to God? What happened?

Ultimately God has the best things in mind for your life, including a desire to use you for great purposes. As Jonah's example shows, obedience often isn't easy because your human nature has a tendency to be rebellious. But by focusing on God's direction provided through Scripture and prayer, you will be led and strengthened in your obedience—and will be blessed.

Jonah 3:1-10 and James 1:22-25

• What happened when Jonah was obedient to God's word? Was the result what God wanted?

• According to James, understanding and obeying God's word leads to blessings. In what is God asking for your obedience right now?

According to Jesus' own words, your love for God is shown through obedience. Jesus used his life as an example for you by pointing to the intimate relationship between loving his heavenly Father and doing exactly what the Father commanded him to do. As you obey God, you validate your love for Jesus himself.

John 14:15-31

• Write in your own words Jesus' explanation about obedience showing love for God.

• If Christ reviewed your last week right now, would he see evidence of your love for him through your obedience?

wednesday

_____
_____
_____
_____
_____
_____
_____
_____
_____
_____
_____
_____
_____

Obedience not only shows your love for God, it also shows your trust. When you believe that God has your best interest at heart, then you are more likely to obey God's commands. Even when you don't quite understand what God is doing or wanting from you, obey anyway—and God can lead you to a new level of trust.

Luke 5:1-11 and Genesis 6:13-22

• How did Peter and Noah each respond to instructions they may not have understood? How do you think their faith grew when they each saw the results of their obedience?

• Think of a time God has called you to obey, even though you weren't certain what could be up ahead. How did it turn out?

thursday

_____
_____
_____
_____
_____
_____
_____
_____
_____
_____
_____

It is when you begin to live obediently, according to the words of Christ, that you find your life full of good fruit and the ability to withstand whatever storms may come. Obedience to God does not promise a life without challenges. But well-practiced obedience will keep you strong when the unexpected happens and will guide you to victory.

Matthew 7:15-29

• What are the ramifications of putting or not putting Christ's words into practice?

• From today's reading, which kind of house best describes you?

One sure way to begin to learn what God wants of you is by reading the Bible, God's instruction book. It's very clear through the pages of Scripture what kind of behavior God finds pleasing and what behavior God views as disobedient. The Psalms can provide you with basic guidance as you develop a lifestyle of obedient choices.

Psalm 119:9-16, 33-40, 57-64, and 97-104

• List all the steps of obedience the psalmist named that you can take to please God.

• Choose one of the ways you listed as your next step of obedience. What will you specifically do to take that step?

_____

_____

_____

_____

_____

_____

_____

_____

_____

_____

What Is God's Great Goal For My Obedient Life? **saturday**

God has another greater purpose for your obedience—to bring others into the kingdom of God. It is only when you become an obedient servant that God is fully able to use you to minister to others. As your life reflects obedience and trust in God, those around you will be encouraged in their own faith. And your practice of obedience will ultimately render you a masterful instrument of God's will.

Acts 3:1-10 and 4:1-22

• What gave Peter and John the courage to stand up to the Sanhedrin (religious leaders)? What was their reaction to Peter and John's boldness?

• Just as God used Peter and John's obedience, God can use your obedience to bring healing and hope to others. Who are you in a position to encourage by your obedient example?

_____

_____

_____

_____

_____

_____

_____

_____

_____

_____

the word on...
SECOND CHANCES

sunday
Where Does The Opportunity For A Second Chance With God Begin?

When you first affirm your need for Jesus, accept Christ, and come into a new eternal relationship with God, you have taken advantage of God's biggest "second chance" opportunity. Following Jesus, however, means a lifelong journey made up of multiple conversions (points of surrender or second chances) that continually transform you into Christ's image. In today's reading, Peter demonstrates a need for conversion that would align his human understanding with the perspective of God.

Matthew 16:13-28

• What type of messiah (savior) does it appear Peter was expecting, and how did Jesus change Peter's perspective?

• What in verses 24-28 challenges your understanding of what it means to follow Jesus?

What If My Need For A Second Chance Is The Result Of Turning My Back On God?

monday

Peter, along with James and John, was one of the persons closest to Jesus during his time on Earth. Not only did Jesus suffer false accusations, beatings, and a cruel death, but he also endured the emotional pain caused by the desertion and betrayal of his friends. By giving Peter a second chance, Jesus sent a clear message: following Jesus is about unconditional love, restoration, and usefulness in the lives of others.

John 18:15-27 and 21:1-19

• Along with giving Peter a second chance, with what did Jesus entrust him (John 21:15-17)?

• Like Peter, when have you experienced a new second chance through listening to Jesus' instructions and following them (John 21:1-11)?

What Can I Expect From Jesus When I Ask For A Second Chance?

tuesday

Unlike a judgmental human perspective, Jesus offers you grace (unconditional, unearned love), cares about you personally, identifies with you without excusing your sin, offers you forgiveness, and leads you out of guilt and condemnation into a changed life. Even in your brokenness you can approach Jesus boldly, confident of receiving understanding and help through another life conversion.

John 8:2-11 and Hebrews 4:14-16

• What was Jesus' attitude toward the woman in today's verses? What did Jesus tell the woman to do?

• A changed life comes from Jesus' grace and restoration combined with your commitment to follow Jesus in obedience. How is Jesus asking you, like the woman, to go and sin no more?

wednesday

God values every individual and is willing to do whatever it takes to bring each person to a restored relationship with God and others. As one who has been changed through a relationship with God, you become a messenger of God's powerful love and forgiveness to those who also need to be reconciled to God and one another.

Luke 15:1-10 and 2 Corinthians 5:17–6:2

• In today's verses, to what extreme did the owners go to restore their losses? What happened when what was lost was found?

• Think of a time when you felt "lost" as an individual, a family member, or a follower of Jesus. Whom or what did God use to restore you?

thursday

The characters in today's Scripture readings illustrate two common attitudes that prevent a conversion: self-centeredness and self-righteousness. But an enthusiastic openness to forgive an offense, coupled with a humble willingness by the offender to confess the offense and ask for forgiveness, creates the formula for a God-inspired second chance at relationship.

Luke 15:11-32

• Describe the attitudes of the father and each of the two sons. How did each attitude contribute to the outcome of the situation?

• Identify a current personal situation of yours in which attitude adjustments are needed to bring about reconciliation and restoration. What do you need to do?

Followers of Jesus are redeemed, broken people on the road to wholeness. Your relationship with God is not based on your sinlessness but solely on the ongoing forgiveness God offers you through Jesus' sacrificial death on the cross. As you face and acknowledge each sin, God immediately forgives, purifies, and empowers you with a new chance to walk in the light—and you will be gradually transformed into the image of Christ.

1 John 1:5–2:2 and Isaiah 55:6-13

• What does "walking in the light" look like? What has God provided to help you keep walking in the light?

• Even those serious about walking in the light experience times of disobedience. What are your most tempting distractions?

Like the illness of the man Jesus healed at the pool of Bethesda, separation from God may have become a lifestyle for you, resulting in a sense of hopelessness about ever being restored. The truth is that as soon as God hears from you that you want to be well (whole), God begins addressing your deepest needs and will give you power to live anew.

John 5:1-15 and Psalm 130

• What was the significance of Jesus' last statement to the healed man in John 5:14?

• What statements from Psalm 130 challenge you to be proactive in asking for a second chance rather than just letting things go?

the word on...
SHARING YOUR FAITH

sunday

Do I Really Have To Share My Faith In Jesus Christ With Others?

_____

_____

_____

_____

_____

_____

_____

_____

_____

_____

_____

_____

The answer to the question is yes! Even though talking about Christ to others can feel intimidating, you are not the only one in this position. From the time of the first disciples until now, all followers of Christ have been called to go into their world and be witnesses to all that Jesus has done. Jesus promises you the power to share your faith.

Matthew 28:16-20 and Acts 1:1-9

• According to Matthew, what specific instructions did Jesus give his disciples as he commissioned them as witnesses?

• In Acts 1:8, Jesus promised his followers spiritual power to witness for him. In what life setting will you commit to share about Christ, beginning today?

It is truly amazing that God allows you the opportunity to be a part of the process of salvation in others' lives through sharing your faith. In fact, if you don't tell others about Christ, they may never hear about or know Jesus. Just as another person initially influenced you for Christ, you too have the great blessing of being a vital link between God and those around you.

Romans 10:8-17
and 2 Corinthians 5:11-21

• "How beautiful are the feet of those who bring good news!" (Romans 10:15). What do you think was meant by this statement?

• The job of an ambassador is to represent someone or something. How well do you represent Christ in your current situation at home, at work, or when you are with your friends?

In today's two passages in Acts, both Peter and Paul give stirring testimony about the work and life of Jesus Christ as they preached to those around them. In these sermons is found the basic gospel message that the first apostles shared and that you can use in sharing Christ with others.

Acts 10:34-48 and 13:13-39

• Summarize in your own words the gospel message that Peter preached at Cornelius's house. What about Jesus did Paul emphasize to his listeners?

• What part of the good news about Jesus resonates with you the most? With whom could you share it?

wednesday

_____

_____

_____

_____

_____

_____

_____

_____

_____

_____

_____

Sharing the message of Christ is not necessarily the same as sharing how Jesus has affected your life. Sharing your faith puts you in the middle of what Christ has done for you personally. Paul did this effectively as he told what happened to him when he met Christ for the first time. It is important to share the basic message of Christ, but that message becomes much more powerful when woven into the personal faith story of Jesus in your own life today.

Acts 26:1-29

• Describe how Jesus changed Paul's life and direction.

• What is your story about how Jesus has personally changed your life?

thursday

_____

_____

_____

_____

_____

_____

_____

_____

_____

_____

_____

Some think they must use big theological words and explain difficult spiritual concepts when sharing their faith. However, the most effective means of sharing your faith is simply to tell others what God has done in your life. Your life experience is far more effective than any theological words. Just as the psalmist did in today's Scripture readings, you also can tell others of the awesome works of God in your life and in the lives of others you know.

Psalms 71:14-24 and 145:1-21

• What life experiences inspired the psalmist to tell others about God's power and greatness?

• What was one of the psalmist's main motivations to share his faith in God (Psalm 71:18)? Do you share this motivation?

Having the message of Jesus and a great personal faith story is not enough if you don't also become intentional in reaching out to others for Jesus Christ. Paul proclaimed that believers must do everything possible to get into a position to speak to others about Jesus. The message in today's readings clearly states that it is not about you but about those who need God's saving grace and new life in Christ.

1 Corinthians 9:16-23
and Colossians 4:2-6

• According to both passages, how should you approach your relationship with non-Christians or "outsiders" to the faith?

• How can you make your own conversation "full of grace, seasoned with salt"?

Sharing your faith in Christ is not just something you do on occasion or just when you feel like it. Sharing your faith is a lifelong calling that all believers have been given by the grace of God. The light of Christ that so graciously found you needs to be shared to all those who are lost and searching for that same peace you have been given. It is in reaching others for Christ that you ultimately find your purpose in life.

2 Corinthians 4:1-15

• What encouragement did Paul offer to believers in this passage?

• In what way does God's light shine out through you to those who know you, work with you, or see you on a regular basis?

the word on...
HOPE

What Hope Is There For Me When I Have Doubts About My Faith?

You are not alone if you have had some skepticism about your faith that dims your hope in Jesus Christ. Even in spite of the many eyewitnesses to Jesus' resurrection, Thomas, one of Jesus' twelve disciples, had doubts about Jesus after Jesus was crucified. Jesus, however, specifically appeared to Thomas to reassure him that he was indeed alive. And Jesus will show himself to you to strengthen your faith and hope as well.

John 20:19-30

• Why did Thomas initially not believe that Christ had risen from the dead? What convinced him?

• Have you ever quickly moved from despair to hope? What triggered it?

The Bible is full of persons just like you who have had many questions about faith and hope in God. In today's Scripture story Nicodemus, a religious leader of his day, came with many questions about Jesus, his ministry, and his teaching about the kingdom of God. Jesus not only took time to answer Nicodemus's questions but also instilled a new hope in this religious leader that eventually caused him to become a follower.

John 3:1-15 and 19:38-42

• According to Jesus, what must take place before we actually see and understand the kingdom of God?

• What drove Nicodemus to seek out Jesus? What questions do you bring to Jesus today?

The world puts its hope in many things—money, power, relationships, and even knowledge. However, the only reliable place to put your hope is in God. You can learn a great lesson about hope from the Old Testament's psalms by King David. David did not place his hope in power, skill, wealth, or even his own strength. He knew that true security rests in God alone.

Psalms 25:1-5 and 62:1-8

• List the reasons King David claimed hope in God. What are the promises made to those who trust in God?

• Which promise of God speaks to your desire for hope today?

wednesday

_____
_____
_____
_____
_____
_____
_____
_____
_____
_____
_____

Hope is often most strongly displayed when we are in great need. Today's Scripture tells the story of two totally different individuals whose desperation drove them to hope in Jesus. Something about the mere presence of Jesus brought out hope in those around him, and Jesus never disappointed those who put their trust in him. Jesus has not changed—he calls us to hope in him no matter what need we might have.

Luke 8:40-56

• What were the circumstances that drove both Jairus and the woman to put their hope in Jesus? What lengths did they go through to get to Jesus?

• When has a deep need driven you to look to God for hope? How did God respond?

thursday

_____
_____
_____
_____
_____
_____
_____
_____
_____
_____
_____

Sometimes life takes painful turns, and you may feel like God has abandoned you. Where do you turn when the God you trust seems absent? The Old Testament prophet Habakkuk had to deal with this issue when God proclaimed upcoming hardship on Israel and hope seemed gone. But Habakkuk also knew that even in the midst of life's pain and bleakness, it was only God who could give him the strength and peace to get through it.

Habakkuk 3:1-19
and 1 Timothy 6:17

• Note the images that Habakkuk used to describe God. How did Habakkuk find hope with nothing physical to hope in?

• What can you do on a daily basis to keep your hope and security in God rather than in things?

Hope for a Christian is more than just believing that something will happen. It also propels you forward into faithful action. Peter provided a prime example in today's Scripture. According to Hebrews 6:19, hope is a firm and secure anchor for the soul. True hope provides a faithful confidence that you can do all things in Christ.

Matthew 14:22-36

• What were the distractions that took Peter's eyes and mind off of Jesus? How did Jesus respond to Peter's question and actions?

• What distracts you from keeping your eyes and your hope on Jesus?

_____
_____
_____
_____
_____
_____
_____
_____
_____
_____
_____

When you hope in Christ, you gain the big-picture perspective that there is more to this life than your own selfish wants and desires. As you continue to help build God's kingdom now, always have your eyes fixed on the hope of the transformation God will bring about in you as well as the inheritance you have waiting with God in eternity.

Ephesians 1:15-23, 1 John 3:1-3, and 1 Peter 1:13-15

• From Ephesians 1:18-19, what are the characteristics of this hope to which God calls you?

• What from these Scriptures brings you the most long-term hope?

_____
_____
_____
_____
_____
_____
_____
_____
_____
_____
_____

the word on...
RECONCILIATION

sunday *What Does "Reconciliation" Mean?*

According to the dictionary, the word *reconcile* is defined as restoring harmony or bringing about a resolution. In the Scriptures this word is used to describe God's powerful love brought to Earth through God's Son in order to restore harmony to the relationship between God and God's people. God first set commandments and laws in place to guide God's people to live in harmony with God and one another—and then later provided Jesus as the means to eternal reconciliation.

John 1:1-18 and 3:16-21

• What reconciling role of Jesus (also called "the Word") is explained in today's readings? What was God's motivation?

• What benefits are you offered by receiving reconciliation with God through Jesus Christ?

God's miraculous reconciling power results in amazing demonstrations of uniting the formerly incompatible, healing differences, and transforming impossible situations. Only through the power of God's love, ultimately illustrated through the sacrifice of God's own Son, is peace and harmony among God's creation possible.

Isaiah 11:1-10 and 65:17-25

• What startling manifestations of God's reconciling love are foretold in the prophecy about Jesus found in Isaiah 11?

• How does Isaiah 65, a picture of the eventual fulfillment of God's transformation of heaven and Earth, help you understand God's definition of reconciliation?

Because of your reconciliation to God through Christ, you become a missionary of reconciliation to others around you. The miraculous message of Jesus brings the power of transformation to you—and changes not only how you view others but also your motivation to reach them with the good news of the gospel.

2 Corinthians 5:11-21 and 6:1-2

• What is the message of reconciliation God has called you to be an ambassador to share?

• As a new creation in Christ (2 Corinthians 5:17), what "old" do you notice is now gone from your life and behavior? What "new" has come?

wednesday

_____

_____

_____

_____

_____

_____

_____

_____

_____

_____

_____

The Scriptures are filled with stories of how God's reconciling love is able to heal even the deepest of wounds. Joseph's jealous brothers sold Joseph (who owned a coat of many colors) into slavery. After faithfully persevering through years of resulting hardship, slavery, and imprisonment, Joseph eventually became Egypt's second in command. He used his position of power as an opportunity to offer reconciling love, even to those who earlier sought to destroy him.

Genesis 45:1-28

• How did Joseph explain his ability to forgive and reconcile with his brothers (Genesis 45:4-8)? What additional blessings did Joseph arrange to provide for them?

• Like Joseph, you may have a situation now in which you can serve as a tool of God's reconciling love. What might it be?

thursday

_____

_____

_____

_____

_____

_____

_____

_____

_____

_____

_____

Followers of Jesus who are committed to the ministry of reconciliation in the world find that such a way of life is challenging. You will be tempted to take the easy route, or become distracted with priorities that are less demanding. At times taking a stand on behalf of justice and fairness for those who are oppressed may come with a price. But God always brings a great harvest when seeds of reconciliation are planted.

Mark 4:1-20

• How is the farmer sowing seeds in various soils like a believer who seeks to bring loving reconciliation to those around him or her? Explain.

• On a scale of one (not very) to ten (very), how persistent are you as you plant seeds of reconciliation in difficult situations? How can you improve?

Jesus taught his followers about the necessity of practicing reconciliation, explaining that unresolved issues must be dealt with even before worshiping God. The Apostle Paul also insisted that relational differences were not to be ignored. Putting on the "new self" in Christ brings a responsibility to carry out reconciliation in every phase of living and helps you mature spiritually.

Matthew 5:21-26
and Ephesians 4:21-27

• What did Paul mean by the statement, "Do not let the sun go down while you are still angry"? Otherwise, how might that give the devil a foothold?

• What speaks to you most strongly from today's readings? Name at least one action step you'll take today.

Jesus brought you the ultimate reconciliation with God through his death and resurrection. But even if you have accepted Christ as your Lord and Savior, it is essential to keep your spirit pure and your conscience clean before God on a daily basis. The Bible teaches about the importance of repentance and asking for forgiveness whenever you stray from obedience. Otherwise, your lack of reconciliation with God will show itself in how you treat others.

1 John 1:8-10 and 2:1-11

• What do today's readings identify as the steps to stay reconciled with God as a follower of Jesus?

• When you have not gotten yourself right with God, how does it affect how you view and deal with those around you (1 John 2:9-11)?

the word on...
WORSHIP

sunday
What Kind Of Worshipers Does God Seek?

_____

_____

_____

_____

_____

_____

_____

_____

_____

_____

_____

_____

_____

_____

True worship is not about theology, place, or method. It is about a human heart responding to and connecting with the heart of God. To worship is to seek God in an honest and intimate way. Jesus doesn't want his followers to concentrate only on external demonstrations of worship, but on a spirit connection based in honesty and truth as well.

John 4:1-26

• What was the woman's response to Jesus' statements on worship? Why was she trying to keep their conversation on an intellectual level?

• What would Jesus say to you about your life of worship?

True worship is an act of sacrifice and surrender. Fully committing yourself to God changes who you are and your relationship with the One to whom you belong. Coming out of darkness to God's kingdom of light, you no longer need to give in to the world's power that tries to squeeze you into its mold. Offering yourself to God instead sets a standard for those around you.

Romans 12:1-2 and 1 Peter 2:4-10

• What do you think it means to offer your body as a living sacrifice? What would that look like in everyday life?

• Which influence of the world is most likely to tempt you to conform to its pattern? How can you resist this temptation?

Of all the characters in the Bible, David (whose story is told in the Old Testament) is associated most closely with worship. David, the greatest of Israel's kings, sometimes failed God with disobedient behavior. Yet throughout his life he was also known to express his love for God with utter delight and joyful abandonment.

2 Samuel 6:12-23 and Psalm 100

• The ark of the Lord, representing the presence of God, was being returned to Jerusalem after being held by Israel's enemies. Describe the reactions of the different characters in this story to this event.

• David recorded his personal worship by writing much of the Old Testament book we know as the Psalms. In your private worship, are you more like David or his wife Michal? Why?

wednesday — *How Can I Worship When I Feel Doubtful?*

_____

_____

_____

_____

_____

_____

_____

_____

_____

_____

_____

Worship may be the natural reaction to an overwhelming, inspiring experience of God—like the women who met Jesus following his resurrection. But worship becomes a sacrificial act in times of doubt. Like some of the disciples, people around you may influence you to question in what and whom you believe, but true worship means to "go and make disciples" even in the face of your doubt.

Matthew 28:1-20 and Psalm 20

• What difference did the appearance of the resurrected Jesus make to the women at the tomb? To the disciples? What doubts do you think the disciples had?

• In what ways do the opinions of your friends, family, or the media create doubt in your faith? How does worship counteract these influences for you?

thursday — *In What Specific Ways Can I Worship And Honor God?*

_____

_____

_____

_____

_____

_____

_____

_____

_____

_____

Worship is a lifestyle. You are to cultivate the godly qualities implanted within you by the Holy Spirit. Every day give to God the excellent and honorable offering of a life that reflects God's character along with the expressions of love and joy that come from your relationship with Christ.

Ephesians 5:8-20 and Colossians 3:12-17

• From today's readings, what specific behaviors are you to practice in order to show honor and glory to God?

• Which behaviors have already become integral parts of your life? Which behaviors do you need to work on?

Throughout the Bible God's followers are called to a life of holiness and discipline. Through Jesus the grace (unconditional love and acceptance) of God is experienced, and the power to be holy and disciplined comes through the Holy Spirit. Such grace and power, ever present in your life, call for reverent and awe-filled worship.

Hebrews 12:18-29 and Psalm 98

• For what reason are you to worship God with reverence and awe (Hebrews 12:25-29)?

• Psalm 98 urges you to "sing to the LORD a new song, for he has done marvelous things." Write a prayer to God expressing thanks for the marvelous things God has done for you.

Your acts of worship (singing, praying, fasting, and so forth) become hollow when you disregard God's mandate to bring about justice for all people in God's name. It's easy to just go through the motions of "worship" and become distracted by wealth, pleasure, and other pursuits. The call to God's people is instead to practice the sacrifice and surrender of true worship, be transformed into God's image, and live out God's values in the world.

Amos 5:21-24 and Isaiah 58:1-14

• According to today's verses, how are believers to truly worship God?

• What are the results of a life lived in devotion and worship to God, as described in Isaiah 58? Write a prayer asking God to increase these kinds of results in you.

the word on...
COMMUNION

Just as you sometimes find yourself taking part in family rituals without knowing their history, Christians often participate in rituals without knowing their origin or full meaning. Communion, or the Lord's Supper, may be one of these rituals for you. To understand this deep and meaningful sacrament you must first understand the Jewish celebration of the Passover and the Passover meal. It was at a Passover meal that Jesus first gave us the practice of Communion.

Exodus 12:1-13 and 21-30

• What does "the Passover" literally mean, and what did the Israelites have to do to avoid the fate of the Egyptians?

• From what do you need God's deliverance right now?

The Passover was a defining moment in the life and history of the Israelites. This mighty act of God that delivered the Israelites from slavery to the Egyptians was also a renewal of the covenant that God had made with Abraham, Isaac, and Jacob, and to the whole nation of Israel. In order for the people to remember this miraculous act of mercy and God's covenant with them, God instituted a yearly celebration around the great deliverance called Passover.

Exodus 12:14-20 and Deuteronomy 16:1-8

• Why do you think God had the people corporately celebrate this event in a festival?

• You also can celebrate God's miraculous work in your own life today. Choose a blessing to acknowledge and celebrate.

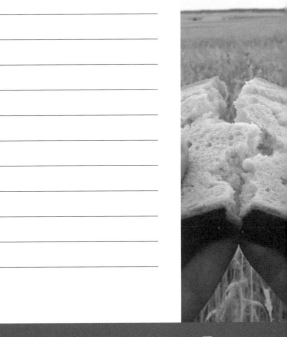

Since God spared from death the firstborn of the Israelites they then belonged to God, and all of them had to be redeemed with a sacrifice to God. These initial offerings to God for sparing their lives, setting them free from slavery to the Egyptians, and redeeming their firstborn were the beginnings of the covenant of law that God made with the Israelites. This covenant also included daily and yearly sacrifices for sins, facilitated by a priest. This was, however, just the foreshadowing of one final, better, and lasting covenant to be set into place through the ultimate sacrifice of Jesus Christ.

Exodus 13:1-16 and Hebrews 7:18-28

• According to Hebrews, how is Jesus different from all of the other priests who served God in the old covenant of law?

• How did sin keep you in slavery in the past? How is Communion a reminder for you of Christ's redeeming love?

wednesday
Why Is Taking Communion Significant For Believers?

_____
_____
_____
_____
_____
_____
_____
_____
_____
_____
_____

The better and permanent covenant that God made with humanity came through Jesus Christ. Jesus came to Earth not only to show us the image of God but also to change physically the covenant of grace that God had with humanity. The Passover celebration was God's representation of salvation and deliverance for the Jews in slavery in Egypt. Christ used that image to show that he was now the physical salvation and deliverance from sin and death for all humankind. The new covenant was no longer in the blood of lambs and bread without yeast, but in Jesus, the Lamb of God.

Jeremiah 31:31-34 and Luke 22:7-23

• What are the characteristics of God's new covenant prophesied by Jeremiah? In what is this new covenant based (Luke 22:19-20)?

• Have you ever sacrificed something for Christ? Describe that experience.

thursday
What Is The Significance Of The Bread Used In Communion?

_____
_____
_____
_____
_____
_____
_____
_____
_____
_____
_____

The two elements believers share in Communion have very specific meanings, both today and in the covenant history of the Israelites. The unleavened bread, which was used during the Passover celebration, symbolized God's quick deliverance of the Israelites out of slavery into freedom. Christ's claim on this bread now is his "body broken for you," clearly representing the ultimate deliverance from sin and death he brought for all people who accept this new covenant. True relationship with God is now found through the sacrificed body of Jesus Christ.

John 6:35 and Hebrews 10:1-25

• Because of the great sacrifice of Christ for us, how does God view you (Hebrews 10:10)? How can you now approach God (Hebrews 10:22)?

• Because you are now in right relationship with God through Christ's great sacrifice, how much time daily will you dedicate to your relationship with God?

The second element used by Jesus at the Last Supper was the cup of wine, which in Jewish tradition was symbolic of blood. Throughout the ancient world blood was always used to seal and confirm all covenants, and it was the same with the original covenant of law that God established with the Israelites. When Jesus took the cup of wine and said, "This cup is the new covenant in my blood," he was sealing a new covenant between God and all humanity, fulfilled by the shedding of his own blood on the cross for our sins.

Ephesians 1:7 and Hebrews 9:1-28

• Name everything the blood of Christ does for humanity, as identified in the Hebrews reading.

• Because you have been forgiven of your sins, what will you do this week to show God gratitude for such great mercy and grace?

Communion is a powerful Christian sacrament because it is a reminder of Christ's sacrifice for us, and it should be observed with humility and reverence. It also offers empowerment to continue living out a life that honors and serves God. Before taking Communion, you as a believer are to examine your life and ask forgiveness for any sin, so that through receiving the bread and cup you may receive God's renewed grace for kingdom living. You have been redeemed by Christ's body and blood and are called to honor him in all you do.

1 Corinthians 11:17-34 and 5:6-8

• According to 1 Corinthians 11, what are the main concerns Paul had with the church's celebration of the Lord's Supper? How are you to approach this sacrament (verse 28)?

• What are some of the ways you can examine your life daily in order to stay obedient to God?

the word on...
FAMILY

sunday

What Responsibility Does The Family Have In God's Intended Outcome For Children?

God has placed an awesome charge and responsibility with the family: to shape the character of children and teach them how to follow Jesus in the everyday world. Mary and Joseph did not neglect Jesus' spiritual up-bringing but honored the charge in Deuteronomy 6 to bring up their child to love, respect, and obey God. They made sure Jesus participated in the faith community, and they found support for their childrearing within this community.

Luke 2:41-52
and Deuteronomy 6:1-9

• According to Deuteronomy 6, what is a major responsibility of the family? What was the result in Jesus' life (Luke 2:52)?

• What was your spiritual upbringing like? How has it affected you today?

Just as parents have a major responsibility to invest in their children, children have a God-given responsibility to honor and respect their parents. Yesterday in Luke 2 you saw that Jesus fulfilled the commandment to honor his earthly mother and father, even though he knew he was the Son of God. In today's world, it's easy to rationalize or ignore the word of God and yield to human traditions and cultural pressure that devalue older adults.

Mark 7:1-23 and Deuteronomy 5:16

• What example did Jesus use to demonstrate the results of an unclean heart?

• Have you ever felt torn between your responsibility to your parents or guardians and to your job, church, or community? What happened?

Families come in all shapes, sizes, and makeups. Hagar illustrated the complex situation of a single mother and the love and care God provides as heavenly Father. Regardless of what your family looks like, God heals, guides, provides for, and sustains those who turn to God.

Genesis 21:8-21
and Psalm 147:1-11

• What did Hagar and Ishmael receive from God? What were they promised?

• Like Hagar, where do you need God's comfort and provision right now?

wednesday

_____

_____

_____

_____

_____

_____

_____

_____

_____

_____

Parenting is a cooperative endeavor between parents and God to bring up a child to be all God created him or her to be. Hannah, a woman who struggled with infertility for years, fully realized that her child was a gift from God. She gave him back to God, releasing him to God's care and call. Although parents may not physically give up a child, they must recognize the need to release emotionally and spiritually that child to God and seek God's guidance in parenting.

1 Samuel 1:1-28

• What do you think Hannah was feeling when she gave up her son? What gave her strength?

• If you have children, what will (or did) you do with them that is the same or different from your parents?

thursday

_____

_____

_____

_____

_____

_____

_____

_____

_____

_____

_____

Spiritual and social development is not confined to the small unit made up of a mother, father, brothers, and sisters. Naomi, mother-in-law to Ruth, drew Ruth to God through a warm and loving relationship. God uses people connected to you through a variety of family relationships to serve as mentors and nurture your growth.

Ruth 1:1-22

• What in Ruth's life changed as a result of her relationship to Naomi (1:16-18)?

• Who has been a person of spiritual influence in your life?

God has provided two families for you: your biological family into which you were physically born and the family of God into which you are spiritually reborn. Jesus himself identified with the spiritual family. God's design was for each family to invest in you as you grow up to be a committed follower of Christ. Even healthy, intact biological families need the influence and investment of the family of God.

Matthew 12:46-50 and 10:32-39

• Who are the members of Jesus' family (12:48-50)? What could separate the members of a biological family (10:37-38)?

• How has following Jesus united or divided your biological family?

Jesus prioritized the well-being of both biological and spiritual children and will hold his followers accountable for their influence on those children. Children learn more quickly from what they see than from what they hear. Adults are encouraged not to grow weary in doing good but to stay the course in choosing how they live before children and in following through with decisions in the best interest of children.

Matthew 18:1-10
and Galatians 6:7-10

• What everyday harmful practices could Jesus be referring to metaphorically through his references to different parts of the body (Matthew 18:7-9)?

• What can reenergize you when you grow weary in doing good, especially in your interactions with children or those who are young in their faith?

the word on...
GRACE

When People Talk About Grace, What Do They Mean?

_____

_____

_____

_____

_____

_____

_____

_____

_____

_____

_____

_____

Grace is the word used to describe the undeserved love and salvation God gives to humans. Grace reflects the helplessness of human beings trapped in sin and disconnected from God. Grace also shows God's willingness and ability to meet your deepest need to be "saved" from your choices to disobey God, and to reestablish the relationship with you that God had in mind from the very beginning.

John 1:1-18 and 3:16-21

• What actions did God take through Jesus to demonstrate love for the world?

• Where are you right now in your understanding and experience of God's grace through Jesus?

The amazing thing about God's grace is that it's free. The Apostle Paul came out of a legalistic, rule-laden, works-oriented background into faith in Christ. And in all of his writings after that, he insisted on this truth of the gospel: eternal life is not the result of rule keeping or works. Your eternal relationship with God comes through simply accepting the love God offers you through Jesus. You can't earn God's favor through good works, but serving God is a natural by-product of receiving and experiencing the love of God.

Ephesians 2:1-10 and Acts 15:1-19

• What "work" were the Jewish believers in Acts 15 requiring of Gentile believers and how did this change to align with the truth expressed in Ephesians 2:8-9?

• Have you ever experienced a time when you felt there was something you had to "do" in order to be loved and accepted by God? What did you do and with what result?

The availability of God's forgiveness and acceptance does not give you a license to sin but gives you freedom to live God's way. As a follower of Jesus you are a walking war zone—with an ongoing battle between your new nature that reflects the goodness of God and your old twisted nature that hungers after every way but God's. An authentic relationship with God is characterized by the growing desire to do life God's way and not take advantage of God's grace toward you.

Romans 6:1-23 and Galatians 2:15-21

• According to Romans 6:22-23, what is the result of a life controlled by your old sinful nature? What benefits come from not allowing sin to reign in your life?

• Today's verses tell you not to be a slave to sin. Where do you feel trapped and need God to set you free through grace?

wednesday

When an imperfect person commits to a perfect God, both failure and success in following God and being formed into God's image are inevitably intermingled. After entering a relationship with God through God's grace, you continue to grow as a follower of Christ by God's grace. The undeserved love, forgiveness, and acceptance of God—not condemnation—make transformation possible and allow you freedom to grow every day through confession and repentance.

Romans 8:1-4 and Psalm 51

• In light of Romans 8:1, how should you handle any feelings of unworthiness and guilt?

• Echoing Psalm 51, write a prayer of confession for the times you have fallen short of complete obedience to God—and write your thankfulness for God's forgiveness and restoration.

thursday

Because of your trust in God's unconditional love and acceptance through Jesus, you have been "justified." That means God sees you "just-as-if-you'd" never sinned. No matter what you have done or where you have been, through Jesus your life is as clean to God as a freshly washed whiteboard, with all your sin erased. Through your experience of receiving God's grace through Jesus Christ you become a demonstration of God's grace to the world.

Romans 5:1-11
and 1 Timothy 1:12-17

• According to Romans 5:8-10, what key words describe what you once were in God's eyes? What did Jesus' death do to change your relationship with God?

• What key words would you choose to describe your life before you were in a relationship with Jesus? What words would describe your life now?

The Apostle Paul mentored many of the first-century Christian churches that sprang up throughout the Middle East, and many of his letters included his prayers for these churches. He wanted each person and every church community to become fully developed in their relationship with God. He knew God's grace was the foundation for all spiritual growth.

Ephesians 3:14-21 and Colossians 1:3-14

• What personal spiritual qualities did Paul pray would develop within each follower of Christ as well as within each church community?

• Which of these qualities do you feel are developing well for you? Which qualities do you need to work on more?

A common thread runs through the spiritual growth pattern of all followers of Jesus: you grow by sharing God's grace with others. The by-product of being undeservedly loved and accepted by God should be to love and accept others, even when they don't deserve it. If you have received the grace of God, live in God's grace, grow in God's grace, and show God's grace to everyone with whom you have contact.

Matthew 18:21-35 and Luke 6:27-36

• What specific actions does Jesus recommend that demonstrate God's grace, especially to those who are difficult to deal with?

• Who in your life right now needs to receive God's grace through you?

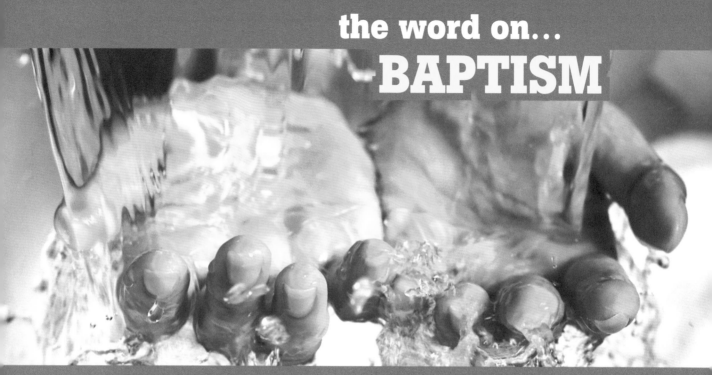

the word on...
BAPTISM

sunday *What Was Significant About Jesus' Baptism?*

_____

_____

_____

_____

_____

_____

_____

_____

_____

_____

_____

_____

John the Baptist's role was to prepare the way for people to respond and follow God's Messiah, calling them to repentance and right living. As Jesus' cousin and childhood friend, John knew Jesus as a righteous man. But even John didn't recognize Jesus as the Messiah until God said so at Jesus' baptism. Jesus (the perfect God/man) did not personally need John's baptism of repentance, but he fully identified with the need of all of humanity to come to repentance and follow God.

John 1:19-34 and Matthew 3:1-17

• According to John 1:29-34 and Matthew 3:16-17, what happened that identified to John who Jesus really was?

• Just as God delighted in Jesus as God's Son, God delights in you. What are any issues that could be blocking your experience of God in this way?

Baptism is the public demonstration of the inward changes that began to happen when you accepted Jesus as your Lord and Savior. Through baptism you show publicly that your intent is to die to yourself and your own selfish agenda and be washed clean through God's forgiveness to live a new life with Jesus. Your old self is "dead, buried, and out of the way," allowing God to transform you anew.

Acts 2:29-41

• According to Acts 2:37-38, what are actions that mark entry into a relationship with Christ? What are the results?

• Repentance and baptism mean you are turning from all other loyalties and affirming allegiance to Jesus. Have you taken these steps?

Contrary to the old covenant of the Old Testament (marked by circumcision), the new life found in Christ and marked by baptism is available to everyone: men and women, Jew and Gentile, slave and free. This new life emerges as you purposefully choose to clothe yourself with (that is, to be like) Christ, so when people look at you they see Jesus. The term "baptized into Christ" does not always refer to the external act of baptism. In today's Scriptures it reflects an intimate bonding with Jesus.

Galatians 3:26-29
and Colossians 2:6-15

• What does intimate bonding with Jesus do for his followers (Colossians 2:9-13)? What is a follower's corresponding responsibility (Colossians 2:6-8)?

• What progress are you making to fulfill your responsibilities as a follower of Jesus?

wednesday

_____

_____

_____

_____

_____

_____

_____

_____

_____

_____

_____

_____

Your baptism, as a sign of your relationship with Christ, is also a sign of your connection with all other followers of Jesus. There is one baptism into one body of Christ. Placing equal value on each individual within the body results in deep, true connection and unity, and is a testimony to the world.

1 Corinthians 12:12-27

• How is each member of the body to be treated? Why?

• Who within the body of Christ is easiest for you to value and affirm? With whom do you need to be more affirming?

thursday

_____

_____

_____

_____

_____

_____

_____

_____

_____

_____

_____

Jesus commanded all of his followers (not just the "professionals") to be involved in winning the lost, teaching and guiding them in their faith, immersing them in everything Jesus taught as they come to the point of their own public statement of faith and develop their own growth pattern. Your life purpose is to take care of Jesus' business of making disciples of people until he returns again. The power to fulfill Jesus' purpose comes through the Holy Spirit.

Matthew 28:16-20 and Acts 1:1-9

• What four things did Jesus command his disciples to do while he was gone? What was his promise in Matthew 28:20 and Acts 1:8?

• Of the four things Jesus commanded his disciples to do, for which one do you need to depend most on the Holy Spirit to empower you?

Even in the Old Testament water was an important symbol for cleansing. Elisha instructed the army commander Naaman to ceremonially wash as part of his healing from leprosy. The water of your baptism symbolizes not only the forgiveness you received when you first accepted Christ but also cleansing of your past history with God as you are saved "through the washing of rebirth and renewal by the Holy Spirit."

Titus 3:1-8 and 2 Kings 5:1-14

• In Titus 3:1-2, Paul lists activities that are good, excellent, and profitable for everyone. What are they?

• In Titus 3, Paul describes the before and after of knowing Christ. What difference has knowing Christ made in your life?

After the promised coming of the Holy Spirit in Acts 2, the disciples spread out over the Middle East, sharing the story of Jesus with anyone who would listen. Philip had a fruitful ministry in winning people to Christ. In chapter 8 of the book of Acts, Philip had two encounters and baptized two people, but with vastly different results. Regardless of your outward participation in baptism, your heart tells the real story.

Acts 8:4-40

• What differences in motivation and understanding of the gospel can you detect that set Simon the sorcerer and the Ethiopian eunuch apart from each other?

• What initially motivated you to seek out Jesus? What keeps you going in your faith?

the word on...
TRUTH

sunday
What Picture Of Truth Does The Bible Give?

Truth: what is accurate, has integrity, is constant, and adheres to fact or reality. Although God's written word—the Bible—is true, all of the truth about God cannot be contained in it. Jesus came to Earth to give the accurate picture of God and demonstrate the reality of who God is and what God is like to a spiritually hungry world. Jesus is the truth of God.

John 14:1-14

• According to what Jesus said in today's Scriptures, identify at least three things that are true about God.

• If Jesus is the way, the truth, and the life, how do you handle claims that there are many ways to God?

Scriptural truth is not an end in itself. God has given you the Bible to make you aware of your need for God and to show you the pathway to God through Jesus. Bible study is an important part of growing as a follower of Jesus. But studying the Bible just to study the Bible, without seeking its true purpose of life transformation, could lead to rigidity and judgment like Jesus experienced through the Pharisees. Faith in Jesus is more than an external belief system; it's a matter of hearing and responding to Jesus from your heart. Studying the truth of Scripture is for transformation, not just information.

John 5:31-47

• How did the Pharisees misuse the information they had from the Scriptures (5:36-40)?

• How has God used your study of the Bible to provide you life transformation?

Those who really want to be Jesus' disciples seek after and handle biblical truth in a vital way. In "knowing" truth, Jesus' disciples go beyond gathering intellectual knowledge to the daily experience of living God's truth. By putting Jesus' teachings into daily practice, his followers seek to cut ties with sin and be set free to live a godly life in the power of his Spirit.

John 8:31-47

• What cause did Jesus give for people's inability to hear him (8:42-47)?

• What truth from today's verses helps you realize you are spiritually set free?

wednesday

ONE W

_____

_____

_____

_____

_____

_____

_____

_____

_____

_____

_____

When Jesus left to return to the Father, the third person of the Trinity became the active agent on Earth. The Holy Spirit inhabits every person who has chosen to follow Jesus. One of the Spirit's responsibilities in your life is to help you understand the ways and truth of God as you open your heart and mind to God. The Spirit will unlock the meaning of Scripture for you and make you sensitive to hearing God personally.

John 16:5-15

• John 16:7-11 lists three ways the Holy Spirit reveals God's truth to the world. What are they?

• Identify a way in which the Spirit of Truth (the Holy Spirit) has revealed a truth of God to you.

thursday
What Does It Mean To Be "Sanctified" By The Truth?

ONE W

_____

_____

_____

_____

_____

_____

_____

_____

_____

_____

_____

On the night before his death, Jesus spent time praying for every person who would choose to follow him— including you! In this prayer Jesus asked the Father to "sanctify" his followers through the truth of God's word. This word means that every follower of Jesus is to be "set apart" for godly living and God's use in the world. Applying and acting on God's truth as revealed in God's word is one means through which sanctification takes place in your life.

John 17:6-19

• In today's Scripture, for what did Jesus ask the Father on behalf of his followers?

• Which of these requests resonates with where you are right now? Write your own prayer, asking God to meet your needs today.

On some level, every follower of Jesus is a teacher because people are constantly observing and learning from your life. Your responsibility is to grow in intimate knowledge of the written word and of Jesus, the living Word, so the truth becomes an integral part of you and you illustrate God's truth to others. In today's verses, Paul coached Timothy (and all believers) on how to live the truth so every follower can lead others into the lifestyle God's truth produces.

2 Timothy 2:14-26

• List the specific things Paul coached Timothy to practice (and avoid) in order to demonstrate God's truth through a godly life.

• What part of Paul's advice do you need to follow more closely?

John wrote this letter in the first century to warn his readers about false teachers and false information. Many teachers in the world claim to know truth, but it is as important to know the truth today as it was in the first century. John clearly distinguished between those who verbally claim to know God and those who show God and God's truth through their actions of love. Tapping into the strength of God's "word that lives within you" gives you the resources you need to walk in the light and live in God's truth.

1 John 2:3-14

• How is truth seen in Jesus and those who follow him?

• Are you living completely truthfully in every area of your life?

sunday
What Was The Relationship Between Jesus And The Holy Spirit During Jesus' Time On Earth?

By taking on human form, Jesus became the example of how to live by faith. Setting aside his power and position as God, Jesus took "the very nature of a servant, being made in human likeness" (Philippians 2:7). In other words, Jesus chose to live on Earth as you are called to live, with all the limitations of being human and totally dependent on the power of the Spirit. Through the Holy Spirit, God promises to empower you to live an obedient and Christlike life.

Luke 4:14-20
and Philippians 2:5-13

• According to Luke 4:14 and 18, what is the source of Jesus' power?

• Review Philippians 2:5-8. How would things be different if you chose the same type of humility and dependence on the Spirit that Jesus did?

While on Earth in human form, Jesus could only be with a certain number of people. Following Jesus' death, resurrection, and ascension into heaven, the Holy Spirit was sent to live within each of Jesus' followers. This allowed Jesus' influence to increase exponentially throughout the world. Jesus can touch the world through you via the Holy Spirit who "lives with you and will be in you."

John 14:15-31

• What role is the Holy Spirit to play in your life (14:25-26)?

• In what do you need a greater amount of peace (14:27)?

Pentecost was a festival celebrated in the Old Testament to honor the grain harvest. Bringing thousands of Jewish families to worship at the temple fifty days after Passover (and Jesus' death and resurrection), this festival created a great audience to witness the sign of the new relationship God would have with humanity. No longer was the Spirit limited to specific individuals; the promised power of God through the Holy Spirit was unmistakably poured out on all who were in relationship with Jesus! This event marked the beginning of the vital community of Spirit-filled individuals (the church) that stretches through the centuries to today.

Acts 2:1-21

• Peter explained to the crowd that the prophecy from Joel 2 was being fulfilled. What did Joel say would happen as a result of the coming of the Spirit?

• When did you first become aware of the power of God's Spirit in your life? What happened?

Having the Holy Spirit living within you does not automatically mean you are filled with the Spirit. To be "filled" means you are controlled and empowered by the Spirit. As expressed by Paul in Ephesians 5, being filled with the Spirit is more than a suggestion; it's a command you are expected to obey. Filling involves confession of any known sin, repentance, and total surrender to God. Ordinary people, filled with the Holy Spirit, demonstrate the extraordinary works of God. Notice the Spirit-filled responses of Peter and John to the threats of the religious leaders in this Acts passage.

Acts 4:1-37 and Ephesians 5:17-18

• What results of being filled with the Spirit were apparent in the New Testament community (Acts 4:32-37)?

• When you are faced with a crisis like Peter, John, and the entire New Testament community faced, what kind of prayer can you utilize from their example (Acts 4:23-30)?

As you read through the Bible, the presence of the Holy Spirit is evident from Genesis 1, when the Spirit was actively involved in Creation, all the way through Revelation 22, the last chapter in the Bible. In the Old Testament, the Holy Spirit was given to specific persons at certain times for particular tasks. Today's verses describe the anointing of David to be king of Israel and the involvement of the Holy Spirit with David's call and responsibility.

1 Samuel 16:1-23

• What important quality was the Holy Spirit prompting Samuel to look for in the next king of Israel (16:7)?

• God is looking for persons today who will influence others for God's purpose. To whom is the Holy Spirit calling you to reach out?

When you approach the Bible, you bring your way of thinking with you. As a product of the culture in which you were born, the family that raised you, and all of your life experiences, you have developed a human perspective that influences your thinking. God's way of thinking is very different. Today's passages will challenge you to surrender your own perspective and seek God's instead. Through the Holy Spirit you can gain "the mind of Christ" and the potential to understand the deep thoughts of God.

1 Corinthians 2:1-16
and Isaiah 55:6-11

• From today's verses, list the differences the Holy Spirit makes in understanding the things of God.

• What could you apply from these verses to move you further in your spiritual maturity?

Everyone who belongs to Christ has the Holy Spirit living within them, and a battle line is drawn between the Spirit and your old sinful nature. Who will win control of your thoughts, attitudes, beliefs, and actions? Only you can choose which way you will live: either led by the Spirit or gratifying the desires of your sinful nature.

Romans 8:5-17
and Galatians 5:13-26

• Create a list of at least eight things from today's Scripture passages that are characteristic of a life controlled by the Holy Spirit.

• What fruit of the Spirit do you desire the most at this time (Galatians 5:22-23)?

the word on...
ROLE MODELS

sunday
What Is My Role In Being An Example For Others?

The call to be a role model for others is clear throughout Scripture. God raises you up in faith not just to look out for yourself but also to build others up in their faith. You are called to live out your life so that those around you may be strengthened in their walk with Jesus Christ. Just as Barnabas strengthened and encouraged Saul, you too must look to build up other believers.

Acts 11:19-26
and 1 Corinthians 10:23–11:1

• From today's passages, list all the ways you are called to strengthen your sisters and brothers in Christ.

• Who first taught you about Christ and was a role model for you?

One of the most important tasks of each generation is to be a witness of God to the next generation. You are called to pass on the faith to your children, to young people in your sphere of influence, and to those persons God places in your life for you to mentor. In passing on this faith you not only secure that the next generation will know Christ; you also launch new missionaries to take Christ to the world.

Deuteronomy 11:2-7, 13-21, and 2 Timothy 1:3-14

• According to Deuteronomy, why was Moses so insistent that the Israelites pass on their faith in God to the next generation?

• Who now looks to you as a positive Christian model?

If you don't pass on your faith in Christ or if you are a poor Christian role model, the outcome can be disastrous. Read how the second generation of Israelites in the Promised Land quickly forgot God and how Eli's sons failed as high priests to honor God—and the results. All believers carry the responsibility to honor God, not only for our children's sake but also for the sake of future believers as a whole.

Judges 2:10-15 and 1 Samuel 2:11-18

• What were the consequences of the Israelites' idolatry in Judges 2? What was the outcome of Eli's poor modeling of godliness to his sons?

• In what way do you need to honor God better in your life so that others may see and grow in their own faith in God?

wednesday

_____
_____
_____
_____
_____
_____
_____
_____
_____
_____
_____
_____
_____
_____

One of the best ways we can help persons with their Christian walks is to constantly remind them of Jesus and the calling that God has placed on their lives. Even though Joshua was Moses' aide for many years, Moses never failed to encourage Joshua to look to the Lord for his strength and guidance and not to Moses himself. Jesus is the one who makes your faith grow, and you are to continually remind others of this truth.

Deuteronomy 31:1-8
and Hebrews 11:32–12:2

• In what ways do Moses and the author of Hebrews encourage you to look to God for power and strength?

• How will you specifically keep your eyes on Jesus throughout the day today?

thursday

_____
_____
_____
_____
_____
_____
_____
_____
_____
_____
_____
_____

One of the greatest role models in the Bible was Mordecai with his niece Esther. Mordecai raised Esther and modeled for her how to live an upright and godly life in one of the toughest times in Jewish history. Not only did Esther follow Mordecai's example but she also willingly put her life on the line for her people. Just like Mordecai, Paul, and Timothy, your example as a believer is crucial to the growth of many in your sphere of influence.

Esther 2:5-7, 17-19; 4:1-17;
and 1 Timothy 4:11-16

• How important were the values that Mordecai instilled in Esther?

• According to 1 Timothy, name the ways you can set a powerful example for those you know.

One of the most amazing aspects of being a Christian role model is inspiring younger believers to do the ministry and work of God themselves. It was through Elijah's life and ministry that his young assistant Elisha was inspired to become a great prophet like his teacher. And it was Paul's life, teaching, and charge to Timothy that launched Timothy to continue to build the young church after Paul's death.

2 Kings 2:1-22 and 2 Timothy 4:1-8

• What was Elisha's request of Elijah before he was taken away?

• List the things that Paul instructed Timothy to do as a minister of God. How do these instructions also apply to you?

How Do I Care For Those God Has Given Me To Shepherd? **saturday**

When you discover that this Christian life isn't about you—it's about helping others grow in faith and purpose—then God will give you great influence. When you come to understand this, you'll faithfully structure your life for the betterment of God's people. Scripture equates this to being a shepherd—one who feeds, guides, protects, and cares for the sheep.

Acts 20:17-35 and 1 Peter 5:1-4

• According to Acts 20:28, who is it that gives you authority to be a shepherd of people? Who is the owner of the sheep you shepherd?

• How can you further structure your life to be the best Christian influence to those God is giving or has given you to shepherd?

the word on...
COURAGE

sunday *What Do I Need To Become A Courageous Christian?*

Courage is most often associated with bravery or confidence, but most of the courageous biblical characters simply saw themselves as obedient to God. These trailblazers were successful because of their strong faith in God, not because they were extraordinarily brave. In the story today, Abram left all he knew and went to a new place simply because God told him to go. In doing so he experienced the fulfilled promises of God and became the "father" of the nation of Israel, the lineage of Jesus.

Genesis 12:1-9 and 17:1-8

• In the Genesis 17 passage, what are the specific promises that God gave Abram because of his faithful actions?

• What step of courageous faith is the next one you need to take?

Today's Scripture is the familiar story of David and the giant Goliath. Whereas David confidently defeated Goliath with a sling and a stone, his courage did not come from his hunting skills. David trusted the power of God, which was what ultimately defeated Goliath and the entire Philistine army. Through David's trust in God the whole Israelite army became more courageous and won a mighty victory.

1 Samuel 17:12-58

• How did David respond to Goliath's taunt in verses 45-46? Why was David so certain he would win the fight?

• What Goliath-like situation in your life do you need to face with God's mighty power, as David did?

God doesn't fix every problem that comes at you by providing a major miracle. Instead, God works in and through you to resolve those problems. Lift up your needs in prayer and seek God's solutions to your circumstances. This will help you be empowered and strengthened in your faith as you learn to rely on God more and more. Like Nehemiah, you too can find courage in praying and receiving God's plan for any situation.

Nehemiah 1:1-4, 2:1-20, and 6:15-16

• Nehemiah outlined to the king a plan to rebuild the wall of Jerusalem (2:1-9). How specific was the plan that God gave Nehemiah?

• How can God use you to be an answer to someone's prayer today?

wednesday

_____
_____
_____
_____
_____
_____
_____
_____
_____
_____
_____

To be a person of courage you must be willing to go wherever God calls you to go. Having godly courage doesn't mean being sure of the future or even feeling in control. Godly courage is following God's call to unknown places or situations, no matter where it might lead. Paul had such courage, and by his obedience to the call he changed the world for Christ.

Acts 22:1-21

• Upon meeting Jesus, what did Paul ask him (verse 8)? What were God's instructions to Paul throughout this passage?

• Have you ever asked God in prayer, "What shall I do for you, Lord?" What happened?

thursday

Does Courage Affect My Leadership?

_____
_____
_____
_____
_____
_____
_____
_____
_____
_____

All godly leadership requires courage. Joshua was called not only to replace Moses as the beloved leader of the Is-raelites but also to lead them in conquering the Promised Land of Canaan. To lead them Joshua was called to be strong and courageous. His successful leadership didn't come from his own power, but from the power that comes as a result of continual obedience to God.

Joshua 1:1-11 and Psalm 138:1-8

• According to Joshua 1:7-8, what was Joshua required to do in order to be successful in his courageous leadership?

• Which of the instructions to Joshua seem meant especially for you right now? Why?

Even in the face of overwhelming odds, you can be a messenger bringing confidence and courage to those around you. All it takes is your trust in the living God who empowers you. Gideon's story is an amazing reminder that victories can happen when infectious courage and faith unite God's people, despite what may seem like lopsided odds from the human point of view.

Judges 6:1-6 and 7:1-25

• Why did God reduce the size of Gideon's army to a mere three hundred men (Judges 7:2)? What was God's role in the defeat of the Midianites?

• What was Gideon's role? Who do you know who needs you to "infect" him or her with your courageous faith and encouragement?

God calls you to be in a community of believers who will help you grow in your faith as well as encourage you to Christian action. One of the important aspects of Paul's success in courageously preaching the gospel all over the Roman Empire was his connection to the church at Antioch. It was in this community of faith that Paul first received his commission to go out as a missionary. He continually came back to them to be strengthened and restored.

Acts 13:1-12 and 14:21-28

• Describe how the church at Antioch chose and sent Paul and Barnabas on their missionary journeys.

• How is your Christian community encouraging you to be a courageous missionary for Christ?

the word on...
HEALING

sunday *What Is Involved In Divine Healing?*

Healing is unquestionably one of the most powerful and compelling themes of the life of Jesus. This week we will explore a variety of stories from the life of Jesus that involve healing. You will notice that one of the common characteristics of a healing encounter with Jesus is a relationship with him. Healing appears to require a willingness to come into closest proximity with Jesus, to call out to Jesus, and to name your need for healing on behalf of yourself or someone close to you.

Mark 10:46-52 and 2:1-12

• Bartimaeus (in Mark 10) was not shy about approaching Jesus. What did he specifically want Jesus to do for him?

• What would your response be to Jesus if he asked you, "What do you want me to do for you?"

Everyone carries issues (from childhood or later) into subsequent stages of life. Some are physical, as with the man at the pool of Bethesda in today's reading, whereas others are relational, emotional, or psychological. The longer you carry your issues the more paralyzed, beaten down, and hopeless you become. The question is: Do you want to get well? Your answer opens or closes the door to Jesus' healing power in your life.

John 5:1-15

• What excuse did the man give in response to Jesus' question (verse 7)?

• What excuses do you need to set aside in order to take your first step toward healing difficult life issues?

A healing encounter with Jesus involves faith that Jesus is capable of healing and will act on your behalf. Jesus demonstrated on multiple occasions his personal authority and power over illness and death itself. Today's stories include two people who showed ultimate faith in Jesus, knowing that just a word or touch from Jesus would be enough.

Mark 5:21-43

• The synagogue ruler and the woman with the issue of blood waited until all other options had run out before they contacted Jesus. In what had they put their faith instead?

• Jesus told Jairus, "Don't be afraid; just believe" (verse 36). In what circumstance do you need to take these words to heart and place your faith in Jesus to act?

wednesday — How Does Jesus' Healing Continue Today?

_____

_____

_____

_____

_____

_____

_____

_____

_____

_____

_____

Jesus told his followers in John 14:12 that following his departure from Earth they would do what he was doing and even greater things. The Holy Spirit, dwelling in the lives of all followers of Jesus, carries on Jesus' presence on Earth. The Spirit continues Jesus' healing ministry within each follower to bring life transformation. The Spirit also uses believers to bring about physical, spiritual, and emotional healing for others in Jesus' name, especially those with the spiritual gift of healing.

Acts 3:1-16

• According to Acts 3:16, what brings about healing?

• As a follower of Jesus, with whom could you share what you have—the hope that comes with a relationship with Christ?

thursday — Why Are Some People Healed And Others Are Not?

_____

_____

_____

_____

_____

_____

_____

_____

_____

_____

_____

A healing encounter with Jesus includes trust that God's bigger plan is constantly at work on your behalf. God's primary desire for you is your spiritual healing through a relationship with God—and that may or may not include physical health and well-being. For some, physical healing is the pathway to a mature relationship with God and transformation into God's image. For others, physical infirmities might be the route. In any and all circumstances God is always at work with a greater purpose in mind.

2 Corinthians 12:1-10 and Romans 8:28-39

• What was God's purpose in not answering Paul's prayer to have his "thorn in the flesh" removed?

• When God appears to be silent concerning an urgent request from you, how do you normally react? How can you develop trust in God during those times?

The Bible does not provide an exact formula for guaranteeing a certain response to your requests for healing. However, it does offer guidelines about how to pray in order to give God's healing power optimal room to work. You can pray alone or with others, but having a pure and godly heart that is focused on God's perfect will is fundamental. Most important is leaving the results to God, who is able to do far beyond all you could ask or think.

James 5:13-16
and Philippians 4:6-7

• How are members of the body of Christ to participate in the healing of others? What guidelines does James present?

• Following Paul's guidelines in Philippians 4:6-7, write a prayer about a situation that needs healing, and release your anxiety to God.

Jesus told the ten lepers in today's story to "go, show yourselves to the priests" and be certified as healed and clean according to the Old Testament law. They stepped out in obedience to Jesus, even before they could physically see their healing, and "as they went" they were healed. Your call is to walk in obedience to Jesus, trusting his work is being completed within you—and give thanks for it.

Luke 17:11-19 and Psalm 103:1-6

• What attitude are you to have as you ask God for healing?

• What do you find most challenging about the concept of healing? Why?

the word on...
WORKPLACE WITNESS

sunday *How Can I Be A Witness At Work?*

_____

_____

_____

_____

_____

_____

_____

_____

_____

_____

_____

It is easy to put your work and your worship into separate areas of your life, but God calls you to be just as strong a witness at work as you are at church. In fact, hard work sets an example for others and gains respect from coworkers. In today's readings, Paul set the standard for "work witnessing" by calling all to work hard and to become spiritual workers God can use.

2 Thessalonians 3:6-15
and 1 Thessalonians 2:6-9

• What were Paul's instructions to the Thessalonians about how to be an effective witness in the workplace?

• Make a list of individuals in your workplace for whom you can pray regularly.

God gives all of us natural abilities and wants us to use these skills for God's own purposes. Some mistakenly think that God only uses spiritual gifts to help build the church, but that's not the case—your workplace skills can also contribute to God's kingdom. When you allow God to use your natural abilities or workplace skills, amazing things can happen. Bezalel and Oholiab were two such individuals; through the power of God they were able to use their skills for God's honor.

Exodus 31:1-11, 36:1-7 and Proverbs 22:29

• What did God call Bezalel and Oholiab to do? How were they able to accomplish these tasks?

• How have you used your skills for God's purposes in the past? What might be some new ways God can use your gifts, skills, and passions to further the Kingdom?

God calls you to be a faithful, responsible, and trustworthy worker wherever you find yourself. Whether your role at work is small or large, God is always looking for faithful, diligent believers in every workplace to whom much spiritual influence can be given. Joseph's life paints a perfect picture of a faithful worker, who by being trustworthy in small roles was elevated by God to literally save much of the known world from starvation.

Genesis 39:1-6, 20-23; 41:41-57

• In Genesis 39, what words are used to describe Joseph's work? To what position did God elevate Joseph because of his faithfulness?

• In what ways are you trustworthy at your workplace? In what do you need to improve (time management, efficiency, integrity, language, and so forth)?

wednesday

How Do I Keep My Work Priorities In The Right Place?

_____
_____
_____
_____
_____
_____
_____
_____
_____
_____
_____

One of the ways you become a better worker is to realize that you are really just a steward of God's world, not an owner of the gifts, talents, abilities, and jobs you have been given. One thing that can help keep your focus on being a faithful steward is remembering that God will one day ask for an account of what you were given. Knowing this, your priority becomes working for the benefit of God and blessing God's people, not just fulfilling your own selfish wants and desires.

Matthew 25:14-30

• What happened to the servants who worked and gained more for the master? What about the one who didn't do anything with the talent he was given?

• How will you stay focused on the truth that you are a steward instead of an owner of your gifts, talents, and abilities?

thursday

What Influence Can I Bring Others As A Leader At My Workplace?

_____
_____
_____
_____
_____
_____
_____
_____
_____
_____
_____

Being an effective witness in the workplace also means having a profound influence on those around you through your actions and reputation. When you live and work trying to fulfill God's purposes God will often elevate you in leadership so that you can have a positive effect on the people around you. It is godly actions and integrity that will bring others to connect with the same Jesus you know and serve.

Luke 7:1-10 and Acts 10:1-48

• How did those around them view both centurions? What kind of influence did they have on those who worked for or served them?

• What kind of influence for Christ would you like to have on those who work for or with you? Write a prayer asking God to help you grow in your maturity of workplace witness.

To be an influence at your job and in your community, you must be a person who constantly maintains a noble character. Our reading today describes a wife of noble character and how she worked both in and out of the house bringing life, abundance, and the blessings of God to her family, her community, and to those who saw her works and actions.

Proverbs 31:10-31

• List or describe the attributes or characteristics of the woman in Proverbs 31. How do those around this woman (her children, her husband, her community) view her?

• Which characteristics of this woman do you have? Which do you need to ask God to develop in your character?

Since our life's work is also our worship, never underestimate how God will use you to build the Kingdom. God's calling to all believers is to do eternal work, no matter what your current job happens to be. Constantly pursue God's best will and purpose for your life. Your goal is to be best positioned by God to help build up the lives of all those around you and point them to Jesus. That is your daily calling in work and witness.

John 6:27
and 1 Corinthians 3:10-15

• What kind of work do John (John 6:27) and Paul (in 1 Corinthians) say will endure?

• What message regarding your daily work do you find in today's readings?

the word on...
A CONTAGIOUS LIFESTYLE

What Was The Apostle Paul's Everyday Method Of Sharing Christ With Others?

_____
_____
_____
_____
_____
_____
_____
_____
_____
_____
_____
_____
_____
_____
_____

In today's Scriptures Paul focused on sharing his faith in Jesus with the Thessalonians and went out of his way to eliminate any attitudes or actions in his life that could possibly contradict his message. Paul demonstrated honesty, not flattery; gentleness, not power; and care for the Thessalonians, rather than fulfilling his own agenda. Through his example he motivated the Thessalonians to respond to Jesus and live a life worthy of him.

1 Thessalonians 2:1-13

• How does Paul describe someone who is effective in sharing his or her faith?

• Are the characteristics Paul lists reflective of your life? What needs to improve?

God's word to God's people, in both the Old and New Testaments, has always been to "love one another." God's people are to care for their neighbor as they themselves want to be cared for. But Jesus took loving one another to a whole new level when he told his followers to love as he loved—unconditionally and sacrificially—dying to themselves for the benefit of others. Acting with this revolutionary love demonstrates the authenticity of your relationship with Christ.

John 13:34-35 and 1 John 3:11-24

• According to John, what behaviors demonstrate love?

• Whose love has demonstrated the reality of Jesus to you? How?

Your lifestyle attracts pre-Christians through the power, peace, and purpose of Christ that they see within you and are longing to experience. Paul knew living a godly life, although important, was not enough. Paul did not hesitate to verbally "testify to the gospel of God's grace" and "proclaim to you the whole will of God" to give pre-Christians the reason for his quality of life. Your Christian walk backs up your talk—and your talk explains your walk.

Acts 20:17-38

• From today's verses, what about Paul's life would have attracted the Ephesians and prepared them for the message he shared? What was his message (20:20-21 and 24)?

• When and with whom is it most intimidating to share your faith in Christ?

wednesday

_____

_____

_____

_____

_____

_____

_____

_____

_____

_____

_____

When Jesus calls you to be an example of life transformation to others, it doesn't mean you have to have all the answers or be perfect. It's not about performance but about living in a relationship with Christ in which you know you are loved and accepted unconditionally. All Jesus asks is for your heart (the center of your being) to be sold out to him, and he takes it from there. Out of a heart focused on God come godly actions. Even when you make mistakes your intentional relationship with Christ serves as a demonstration of God's unconditional love and acceptance, and that attracts others to God.

Luke 6:43-45 and Matthew 7:15-23

• According to today's verses, what are the by-products of a true follower of Jesus?

• What aspects of your Christian lifestyle clearly back up what you say and believe? In what areas could you improve?

thursday

_____

_____

_____

_____

_____

_____

_____

_____

_____

_____

_____

God's economy is to let nothing go to waste. God uses every part of your life experience to benefit you in character development and to give hope to others. Because you have walked through troubling times and experienced God's presence and power, you can understand and come alongside someone in a similar situation and point him or her to the hope that comes from Jesus.

2 Corinthians 1:3-14

• What was Paul's purpose in sharing his trials with the Corinthians (1:9-11)?

• With whom could you give hope by sharing your story?

Because you are a follower of Jesus, you are set apart to be like Jesus. You are to approach others as Jesus would and not "from a worldly point of view." Whereas the world expects judgment and condemnation, you are called to be a reconciler: one who leads others to live in harmony with God. Keep acting in love and speaking hope until those around you are won to God.

2 Corinthians 5:11–6:2

• According to 2 Corinthians 5:11 and 14, what motivated Paul to share his faith?

• What difference has your own experience of God's love made in how you approach others regarding their faith?

In his letter to the church at Ephesus, Paul urged followers of Christ to live together as family and to develop their personal relationships in such a way that pre-Christians would be attracted to the Christian approach to life. By living with a totally new attitude, to which the world is unaccustomed, followers of Jesus demonstrate the character of God.

Ephesians 4:17–5:2

• List at least five behaviors Paul named that are to characterize a follower of Christ.

• Choose one behavior in your list that you will work on changing this week. What is it?

GOD'S CALL

sunday — *Whom Does God Call?*

The "calling" of God can often be confusing. Some tend to think that it only comes to very special persons at special times. But the call of God actually extends to all Christians to do the unique work of God in various places and opportunities. The key is to remember that God has a calling for everyone; you just need to be willing to do the mission you're called to do.

John 15:14-17 and Acts 19:1-19

• What was God's calling for Saul? For Ananias? What has Jesus chosen all of his followers to do?

• Has God ever called you to do a specific task for the Kingdom? Explain.

If you don't know God's calling on your life, it may be because you don't actually know how to hear or recognize God's voice. There are many ways that you can hear God's voice, such as through Scripture reading or through other people. God may occasionally desire to speak directly to you in a still, small voice from the Holy Spirit to your spirit. It is up to you, however, to begin to take time and listen for direction and God's call. Otherwise, like Elijah, the worries and fears of daily life may distract you.

1 Kings 19:1-21

• In what form did the word of God come to Elijah? What was Elijah's response (verses 12-13)?

• What kind of "noise" is keeping you from hearing the voice of God?

Am I Really Good Enough To Be Used By God? tuesday

It is easy to assume that only really "good" persons get to be called by God—when just the opposite is true. All of us are sinners and in need of the grace of God; none of us are really worthy on our own to be God's servants. However, being called is not based on our righteousness but on God's. Isaiah faced this same situation when he encountered God's call on his life. Though Isaiah felt inadequate, God chose him for a challenging task.

Isaiah 6:1-13 and 51:15-16

• What was Isaiah's response to seeing God? What did God do to prepare Isaiah for his calling (verses 6-7)?

• What do you need to do to open your heart to God and say, "Here I am Lord, send me"?

wednesday

If anyone in the Bible was prepared to fulfill the call of God, surely it was Moses, right? Wrong. Moses was a human to whom God literally spoke face-to-face, but Moses didn't have much confidence that he would be able to do what God called him to do. Nonetheless, God used Moses to accomplish amazing miracles and free the Israelites from bondage. Through his many experiences, Moses learned that when God calls, God provides.

Exodus 3:1-22 and 4:1-17

• What specific arguments did Moses use to defend his perceived inadequacies in fulfilling God's call?

• Describe a time God used you despite your shortcomings.

thursday

Scripture shows that God's loving heart is concerned with people. And as you examine the life of Jesus, you can see in Jesus' ministry his incredible, passionate desire was to reach out to individuals, particularly those who were hurting or oppressed. For these reasons, as a follower of Jesus you can be certain that one call God has given you is to serve and help those who are in need.

Isaiah 61:1-3 and Matthew 11:1-6

• How was the calling of Jesus described in the prophecy found in Isaiah 61? In Matthew 11, how did Jesus describe his own calling and ministry?

• How might God be asking you today, in the spirit of Jesus, to be the hands and feet bringing God's love to those around you?

The calling of God is usually not easy or trouble free. When helping the oppressed or persons in need you may find yourself coming up against evil in a rebellious and sinful world. But even in the midst of challenge and persecution you can be comforted that God will ultimately be by your side. Jeremiah and Ezekiel were both called to be God's spokespersons in troubled times.

Jeremiah 20:1-13
and Psalm 143:1-12

• What problems did Jeremiah come up against as God's prophet? What did God promise him?

• Reflect on Psalm 143. How does God keep you strong in the face of opposition as you serve?

At What Age Does God Begin To Call His Followers To Serve? **saturday**

Throughout history, God has used believers of all ages and stages in life—including children and teens. The Old Testament contains the stories of Jeremiah and Samuel, both first called by God when they were very young. No matter what season of life you are in, God desires to use you fully for specific kingdom work.

Jeremiah 1:1-10
and 1 Samuel 3:1-21

• How did God equip young Jeremiah to be a prophet? What was young Samuel's response to God's call?

• What makes your current time of life a good one for God to be able to use you for Jesus' work in the world?

the word on...
RADICAL FAITH

sunday *What Makes Faith Radical?*

According to Webster's New Collegiate Dictionary, the word *radical* means "a: extreme; b: tending or disposed to make extreme changes in existing views, habits, conditions, or institutions." Jesus told Peter in Matthew 16 that this type of faith goes beyond a statement of intellectual belief to doing whatever it takes to live out the will of God. By choosing to commit to God's way daily and closely follow Jesus, you will experience extreme changes as God transforms you into Christ's image.

Matthew 16:13-28

• Describe the difference between Peter's understanding of what it meant to follow Jesus, versus Jesus' definition.

• How is God calling you to exercise the faith that will bring extreme change to your existing views or habits?

When faith in Jesus is clearly demonstrated the response is not usually neutral. People will either applaud you or mock you. They will accept or reject Jesus; and persecution from religious or political institutions, family, and friends can sometimes result. The apostles were imprisoned and beaten to tone down their bold statements of radical faith, but "day after day, in the temple courts and from house to house, they never stopped teaching and proclaiming the good news that Jesus is the Christ" (Acts 5:42).

Acts 5:12-42

• What was the basis of the radical faith expressed by the apostles (Acts 5:29)?

• Have you ever felt persecuted for your radical faith? What happened?

The ability to act in radical faith is grounded in both radical trust and radical obedience. If you keep God as your number one priority, you are guaranteed challenges to risk everything and to make difficult, heart-wrenching decisions. You may battle feelings that tempt you to postpone or completely disregard obedience to God's call. But faith in God's character, love, and provision will empower you to follow through. Acting in obedience makes your trust in God a reality.

Genesis 22:1-19 and Matthew 10:32-39

• How quickly did Abraham respond to God's direction to sacrifice Isaac? What does this say about Abraham's relationship with God?

• When have you obeyed and found God's provision? What was the situation?

wednesday

What Does Radical Faith Have To Do With My Lifestyle?

_____
_____
_____
_____
_____
_____
_____
_____
_____
_____
_____
_____

Radical faith is reflected in the lives of Jesus followers through their character. They demonstrate the actions and attitudes of Jesus even in times of crisis or discouragement and regardless of the influence of their culture. In the Old Testament, Joseph showed godly character in choosing to do right morally, refusing to become bitter or hateful toward those who sinned against him, and always serving with excellence. He looked beyond his difficult situations to see the hand of God at work.

Genesis 39:1-23

• How did Joseph's radical faith in God sustain him (Genesis 39:8-10)?

• What scenario would be most likely to tempt you to compromise morally? What enables you to uphold your commitment to God?

thursday

What Does It Take To Live Out Radical Faith?

_____
_____
_____
_____
_____
_____
_____
_____
_____
_____
_____

Courage is a key component in living out a strong commitment to and faith in God. Practicing radical faith will create situations in which you will need to take a courageous stand for God. Shadrach, Meshach, and Abednego refused to bow and worship Nebuchadnezzar's golden idol, courageously making a public statement of their commitment to God alone and of their trust in God's provision. Their radical faith and God's supernatural deliverance won over King Nebuchadnezzar and influenced an entire nation.

Daniel 3:1-30

• From Daniel 3:16-18, list four things that provided Shadrach, Meshach, and Abednego the confidence for their radical faith and courageous stand.

• How do you stay faithful in challenging times even when you cannot foresee God's intervention?

Every follower of Jesus is at a different point on the faith journey. The good news is that God does not demand perfect faith but works with you individually right where you are. You don't have to have all the answers! Being radically committed to Jesus simply means you have wholeheartedly committed all you currently know of yourself to all you presently know of Jesus. As you allow God to transform you and "help your unbelief" you grow in faith.

Mark 9:14-29

• In Mark 9:21-24, the boy's father verbalized the internal faith conflict many followers of Jesus feel. How did Jesus answer this man?

• In Mark 9:29, Jesus connected faith and prayer. What connection exists between the state of your prayer life and the level of your faith right now?

Jesus was clear when he shared with his disciples that following him would be costly. Each person on Earth is faced with the decision to reject Jesus' invitation and continue life as usual or to respond and follow in total surrender and complete obedience. There is no in-between. Not everyone will make the radical commitment to fix his or her eyes on Jesus, set aside anything that would distract from following completely, and never look back. But for those who do, knowing the cost of what you are committing to helps prepare you to go the distance with Jesus.

Luke 9:51-62 and 14:25-35

• According to Jesus in today's Scriptures, why is it critical to evaluate the cost of following him? What does following him require?

• What excuses are you most likely to use to rationalize and avoid complete obedience to Jesus?

the word on...
GOD'S WILL

sunday — *What Steps Could Lead Me To Knowing God's Will Better?*

_____

_____

_____

_____

_____

_____

_____

_____

_____

_____

_____

_____

If you're like most Christians you want to know what God's will (ideal plan) is for your life, especially when it comes to major decisions you have to make: career choices, relationships, life struggles, even parenting children! According to the Bible, discovering God's will must begin with a strong desire to seek it—not just for big decisions but also in every detail of your life. Second, it's important to read and study Scripture for God's guidance. The third step is to be willing to put into practice the aspects of God's will that become clear to you.

Psalm 119:97-112

• Reflect on today's Scripture reading. According to Psalm 119:100, what brought the author deeper understanding of God's will?

• What steps of greater obedience to God might lead you to understand God's will more clearly?

From a human perspective you may feel as though you are confidently in control of your life and circumstances. But that is only human deception. God is the One ultimately in control! Seeking to do God's will instead of your own often involves a major change in attitude, thought, and perspective. It is through the awareness that true certainty only lies in the hands of God that you can begin to fully trust God in your life and decisions.

Psalm 37:3-7 and James 4:13-17

• According to Psalm 37, what are the steps you can take to put God first? What does God promise in return?

• What aspect of attitude change as described in the James reading do you need to implement?

Through reading about the life and ministry of Jesus you can easily see that he was driven to fulfill God's will in everything he said and did. However, even Jesus—who was God in human form—had to continually seek to know and obey God's will. Jesus accomplished this through his vigorous prayer life and his study and knowledge of the Scriptures, God's word. Jesus is your example to follow if you, too, want to carry out God's will for your life.

John 6:35-40 and Mark 14:32-42

• According to Jesus, what was God's will for his ministry here on Earth? What part did prayer have in the decisions Jesus made, especially near the end of his life?

• What is the difference between seeking God's will and simply asking God to bless your will?

wednesday

_____
_____
_____
_____
_____
_____
_____
_____
_____
_____
_____

Just as Jesus sought God's will and direction in his life by regular communication with God, you as a believer need to do the same. Prayer is the vital key not only to knowing God but also in receiving God's guidance for daily living. King David was known as a man after God's heart because he habitually inquired of God before making decisions and taking action, as he explained in a number of Psalms he wrote. You, too, have this same "open door" into God's wisdom and guidance through prayer.

Psalm 27 and Matthew 6:5-15

• How specific were David's inquiries of God in Psalm 27? What were his expectations of God's response?

• In the Lord's Prayer that Jesus taught his followers (Matthew 6:9-13), what did he include about praying for God's will?

thursday

_____
_____
_____
_____
_____
_____
_____
_____
_____
_____
_____

If you live your life by the principles and truths taught in the Bible, you will be following the will of God. In fact, most of the daily decisions you face can be guided by those principles, especially as taught and lived by Christ himself. However, the Bible is not just philosophy and life teachings. It is a living word that will speak to you in your spirit, where you are, about the unique issues and choices you are living and making each day.

Psalm 19:7-14 and Proverbs 2:1-11

• What are the ways the psalmist described the statutes and precepts (truths) of God? According to Proverbs, what is promised to the person who accepts God's words and wisdom?

• How much time do you spend every day reading the Bible? Does it need to increase?

One of the main purposes of the Holy Spirit is to help lead you in your Christian walk and give you power to live faithfully every day. The Holy Spirit works in a variety of ways. Whether you're being prompted to some kind of action, convicted of a wrongdoing, being led to help someone, or sensing God's presence, the Holy Spirit will guide you if you openly listen for direction. Scripture shows how the Holy Spirit guided Paul in his ministry.

Acts 16:6-10 and Colossians 1:9-14

• How do you gain knowledge of God's will, according to Colossians 1:9? In what ways did the Holy Spirit work in the Acts passage?

• Has the Holy Spirit ever moved you to action? Explain.

God's passion is for the love, wholeness, and welfare of all people. God's will for you is to be the hands and feet of Jesus, bringing good news to the poor, freedom for the prisoner, recovery to the sick, and peace to the oppressed. By serving others in these ways you are fully investing in doing the will of God.

Matthew 25:31-46

• From Matthew 25, list what Jesus described as the work his followers are to do for those in need.

• How have you been the "hands and feet" of Jesus this week? This month? This year?

the word on...
INFLUENCE

sunday   *Do I Really Have Much Influence On Those Around Me?*

_____

_____

_____

_____

_____

_____

_____

_____

_____

_____

_____

_____

_____

God's faithful followers can bring powerful influence for good, especially when encouraging others to make right decisions. Mordecai, the uncle of a beautiful Jewish woman named Esther who became queen, urged her to take the right (though dangerous) stand on behalf of God's people. Esther responded to her uncle's influence, with history-changing results.

Esther 4:6-17, 7:1-10, and 8:1-8

• What strategy did Mordecai use to try to influence Esther? How did Esther use her royal influence on God's behalf?

• Who has recently influenced you to make a right and faithful decision?

No matter what your life history has been, God can use you for strategic good when you surrender yourself to God's plans. The prostitute Rahab acknowledged the God of Israel by allowing her home to become a hiding place, thus enabling the success of God's people. Hundreds of years later even James wrote of Rahab's example. Her willingness to daringly use her influence to serve God's purposes provided the crucial element needed for victory.

Joshua 2:1-24, 6:15-25, and James 2:24-26

• How did Rahab's obedient use of her influence also eventually help her family?

• By aligning yourself with God's plans, what godly influence can you bring to a current situation?

God desires you to be an agent of his positive influence, and at times may even use miraculous means to direct you. The Moabite king Balak desired to destroy God's people, the Israelites. So he summoned a local pagan fortune-teller named Balaam to curse them. By a supernatural circumstance, God prevented Balaam from following Balak's evil influence and then used Balaam as a tool of godly influence to bless the Israelites instead.

Numbers 22:1-38 and 24:1-14

• What did God use to get Balaam's attention (Numbers 22:28-30)?

• What surprising means has God ever used to get your attention and guide you for God's purposes?

wednesday

STAY ON TRAIL

Husband Ananias and wife Sapphira, believers who were part of one of the first Christian communities, negatively influenced each other—with deadly consequences. As a follower of Jesus, you are called to evaluate carefully the advice and influence of those around you, even those who are Christians. Without prayerful guidance from the Holy Spirit, it becomes easy to justify selfish or disobedient behavior—especially when other believers seem to affirm your direction.

Acts 4:32-37, 5:1-11, and 1 Corinthians 2:6-16

• What misguided justification do you think Ananias and Sapphira might have used for their actions?

• According to the 1 Corinthians 2 passage, what have you been given to help you discern God's direction and influence?

thursday
What Kind Of Positive Influence Motivates Others?

Fear and discouragement can influence followers of God to become distracted from the mission. When God called Zerubbabel and Jeshua to lead the rebuilding of God's temple in Jerusalem, they fearfully halted their work for sixteen years because of the threats and lies of enemies. It was only through the motivating influence of prophets Haggai and Zechariah that the rebuilding successfully resumed. They refocused the people on the bigger picture of God's plans and came alongside them in the work.

Ezra 4:1-5, 4:24—5:17, and 6:14-18

• What higher authority did God's people name as their motivating influence to resume rebuilding the temple (Ezra 5:11)?

• Do you know someone to whom you can bring encouraging influence to continue God's work?

God sometimes uses the spiritual influence you bring to others to trigger a chain reaction beyond what you could ever imagine. Stephen, the first early Christian killed because of his faith, ultimately influenced many toward an encounter with Jesus. Even Saul, a devout religious leader who hated Jesus followers, was later part of the spiritual "chain reaction" caused by Stephen's influential witness.

Acts 6:8-15, 7:54–8:1, and 9:1-22

• How did Stephen react to the persecution he received as a result of his faith in Jesus?

• What chain reaction caused by the godly influence of a believer have you ever been a part of or witnessed?

After Lydia accepted Christ and became a believer, she brought her spiritual witness and influence to her entire family. Jesus taught his followers to let the light of their faith shine for all to see, no matter how friends and relatives might respond. Rather than attempting to influence others through judging and condemnation, you are to take the path of love and serve as a faithful example that will point others toward God.

Acts 16:11-15 and Matthew 5:14-16

• What was the first place Lydia evidently took the good news of Jesus to share? What happened?

• Write a prayer asking God for wisdom on how to bring the influence of your faith to those closest to you—how your "light" can shine before them.

the word on...
LEADERSHIP

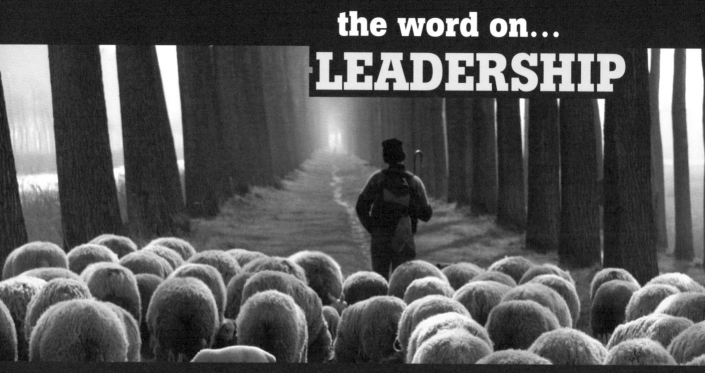

sunday
What Does Being A Believer Have To Do With Leadership?

God calls specific persons into particular leadership roles, but as Christians we are all called to become godly leaders in whatever circumstances we find ourselves. One of the best examples of godly leadership in the Bible is found in the life and struggles of Moses as he led the Israelites out of Egypt and to the Promised Land. And even though Moses initially resisted becoming a leader, his faithful obedience to God was the first step in becoming a leader God could use.

Exodus 14:10-31
and Hebrews 3:1-6

• How would you describe Moses' faith in God throughout the Red Sea story?

• How faithful are you in relying on God's direction in the places you have been positioned to lead?

To be a godly leader you must also become a whole-hearted servant of God. Not only did Moses lead out of faithful obedience, he also knew what it meant to single-mindedly serve God. Godly leadership entails full allegiance to God with all your heart, soul, and mind. Throughout the many trials that Moses and the Israelites endured in their journeys (and even when his siblings were critical), God proclaimed Moses to be "my servant."

Deuteronomy 10:12-13, 34:5-12, and Numbers 12:1-8

• According to Deuteronomy 10, what is asked of persons who truly want to serve the Lord? List them.

• From your list, where are you succeeding and what needs improvement?

Because godly leaders are true servants of God, their calling is to serve people. Though you can serve people in many ways, great leaders continually lift up those they lead in prayer to God. Moses constantly stood in the gap for the Israelites and interceded in prayer for them, even in the worst circumstances. In the second Scripture reading today, see what Paul wrote about prayer to the people he was leading.

Numbers 14:1-20 and Romans 1:8-10

• What was the circumstance in which Moses prayed for the Israelites? What was God's response?

• Do you pray for the people you are serving, leading, or for whom you are working? With what results?

wednesday

_____
_____
_____
_____
_____
_____
_____
_____
_____
_____
_____

Another key way leaders serve people is to teach them the ways of God. One of the most important tasks that Moses performed was to inform the people about God's instructions for living. In fact, Moses became the direct mediator between God and the Israelites and faithfully brought God's word to the community. We now have a new mediator in Jesus Christ, but as a leader you are still given the task to teach people about God's truth and instruct them in the paths of obedient living.

Exodus 19:1-25
and Colossians 3:16-17

• What were some of the ways Moses prepared the Israelites to meet God? Where did Moses get his information?

• Like Moses, in what ways are you first listening to God so that you know how to instruct and encourage others?

thursday

_____
_____
_____
_____
_____
_____
_____
_____
_____
_____
_____

Moses relied completely on God's guidance to help him lead. In today's reading, Moses implored God never to send them forward without the Lord's direction and presence. It was in this guidance from God that Moses found both strength and confidence to lead the Israelites for forty long years.

Exodus 33:7-23

• What were Moses' three requests of the Lord (verses 13, 15, and 18)? What was God's response to each?

• Which of Moses' requests is most essential to you today? Why?

To be a godly leader also means allowing others to come alongside to help you with leadership duties. Moses initially took all the responsibility of leading the people, but soon learned that wasn't a suitable way to get everything completed. He eventually discovered that true leadership distributes and delegates authority to others who are ready and qualified to lead. In fact, true leadership is about raising up persons to do the work of God along with you.

Exodus 18:7-27
and Deuteronomy 1:9-18

• According to Exodus 18:21 and Deuteronomy 1:13, what are the criteria for choosing individuals who can help lead?

• Do you naturally delegate responsibility to others or do you tend to follow the adage "if you want something done right, you've got to do it yourself"?

Moses constantly urged the Israelites to remain faithful to God's call and commands, and knew that as their leader he needed to provide that daily encouragement. You, too, are called to be a daily encourager so that those around you will be reminded and strengthened in their walk with Christ and will remain focused on God. Become an encourager and you will become a godly leader in exactly the life setting in which you find yourself today.

Deuteronomy 4:1-14
and Hebrews 3:12-13

• What were some of the specific ways Moses encouraged the people?

• How does remembering and telling about God's past actions help encourage both you and others?

the word on...
PRIORITIES

sunday *What Is Top Priority To God?*

_____

_____

_____

_____

_____

_____

_____

_____

_____

_____

_____

_____

_____

As a follower of Jesus you are being transformed into Jesus' image through your obedience. During this process Jesus' life increasingly becomes your life and Jesus' priorities increasingly become your priorities. In today's Scriptures, God clearly identifies the priorities God's followers are to have: you are to love God first and foremost; act humbly, justly, and mercifully toward others; and abandon yourself to God, letting God's power and provision flow through your life.

Micah 6:6-8 and Matthew 6:25-34

• From these passages, what is to be most important to followers of God? What is to diminish in importance?

• On a scale of one (cool as a cucumber) to ten (stressed to the max), how would you rate yourself on seeking God and letting go of daily concerns?

Justice is high on God's priority list because people matter to God. Justice goes beyond observing certain worship forms and going through religious rituals. You demonstrate justice by internalizing God's value of doing right by all people and acting on that value. God wants you, as God's follower, to treat others fairly and righteously (as God would treat them).

Mark 12:28-34
and Amos 5:11-15, 21-24

• According to Amos, why did God "despise" Israel's religious feasts?

• Toward whom do you need to think or act more justly?

Operating according to God's priorities takes you beyond the typical behavior of society. Although the norm is to take care of yourself and to base your responses to others on the way they have treated you, God's instruction is to initiate acts of love toward others, whether they "deserve" it or not. God's love and mercy are undeserved and freely offered. As Jesus said, "Be merciful, just as your Father is merciful."

Luke 10:25-37 and 6:27-36

• From these verses, who is deserving of a demonstration of God's love? Why?

• Who in your circle of influence is in need of God's mercy and love? What action will you take?

wednesday *What Does It Mean To Walk Humbly With God?*

_____
_____
_____
_____
_____
_____
_____
_____
_____
_____
_____

God calls for humility in your relationship with God and in your approach to life. To fully live as God intends, you have to come to the realization that life is not about you; it's about prioritizing your relationship with God and fulfilling God's purpose in your life. The challenge is to completely surrender as your life is reoriented to God's value system and worldview.

Luke 18:9-14 and James 4:1-10

• According to today's Scriptures, what are some outcomes of pride (lack of humility)? What solution did James offer in 4:7-10?

• Taking an honest evaluation of your spiritual life, in what areas do you need to humble yourself and surrender to God?

thursday *How Are My Obedience And God's Priorities Related?*

_____
_____
_____
_____
_____
_____
_____
_____
_____
_____
_____

Going beyond listening and studying to applying and acting on what God says will bring changes in every part of your life. Living out God's word authenticates and deepens your relationship with God and others, and changes your perspective on life and faith. Obedience is the key to the transformation process God is working in your life and will result in God's priorities being demonstrated through you.

James 1:19-27

• According to James, what are the results of doing God's word?

• What from this week's Scriptures so far could you purposefully act on today?

Because people matter to God, meeting their needs is high priority to God. Although doing good for others is not the basis of our salvation, it is the result of our relationship with Christ. Those who truly love God will have God's compassion for others. Authentic service comes from serving others as if you were serving Jesus.

Matthew 25:31-46

• What areas of need does Jesus list? What were the two different outcomes for those who served willingly and lovingly and those who did not?

• Are you serving to meet the needs of others in any way right now? How could you become more involved?

Rather than a passive, easy existence, following Jesus and living out God's priorities require stepping out of your comfort zone. Risk, trials, pain, and suffering are components of every life; followers of Jesus are no exception. To successfully navigate all of life requires deep and complete trust that God will lovingly work in every situation to help you grow in your spiritual maturity. The same Peter who stepped out of the boat to follow Jesus later wrote today's passage about enduring suffering in Jesus' name.

Matthew 14:22-32
and 1 Peter 4:12-19

• Who is to be the object of your trust, no matter the situation (Matthew 14:27 and 1 Peter 4:19)?

• In what situation do you need to more deeply trust God to work and to grow your spiritual maturity?

the word on...
REVIVAL

sunday
Is It Unusual To Have Times Of Spiritual Dryness And Distraction?

_____

_____

_____

_____

_____

_____

_____

_____

_____

_____

_____

What Christians have called "revival" describes an experience of spiritual reawakening or revitalization—a deeper reconnection with God. Because you are a fallible human, you may experience occasional seasons in which you need to bring your attention and commitment back to focus anew on your faith. As recorded in the Bible, the people of Israel regularly had the need to be called back to allegiance to God through spiritual renewal, and in today's verses, God used Elijah to do exactly that.

1 Kings 18:16-40

• With what did Elijah confront the people of Israel (18:21)? What was Elijah's purpose (18:37)?

• Are you "wavering between two opinions" and need spiritual renewal? How so?

Josiah became king of Israel at age eight and began his spiritual journey at sixteen. Under his leadership, the temple in Jerusalem was restored and a copy of God's Law (their Bible) was uncovered during its excavation. As he read the words contained in the Law, Josiah immediately recognized how far Israel had slipped from God. Without delay, he led the people in renewing their commitment to follow God alone and to live according to God's commands.

2 Kings 22:1–23:3 and 23:21-25

• What did Josiah do as a result of the insights he gained from the Bible?

• As it did Josiah (22:19-20), what instruction from God's word could give you the peace you crave?

How Should I Handle Overwhelming Situations? **tuesday**

The joy and peace God intends for you as a God-follower is forfeited when you allow overwhelming circumstances and fear to consume you. Your relationship with God is renewed when you look beyond yourself to trust God alone, no matter how dire your circumstances. King Jehoshaphat led the people of Israel to earnestly seek God when they were powerless and did not know what to do. Rather than being afraid or discouraged, they trusted God's provision and praised God even before they knew the outcome.

2 Chronicles 20:1-30

• What revival did God offer the people as God answered their fears through Jahaziel (20:15-17)?

• When have you felt powerless, not knowing what to do, and God came through for you?

wednesday

In 538 B.C., the people of Israel returned from exile in Babylon to their own land, intending to rebuild the temple of God. Instead, they were quickly consumed with their own needs, focusing on building their own houses and developing their food supply. Over the years they abandoned their call to serve God first. Self-centeredness and a lukewarm attitude toward the things of God resulted in a lack of meaning, a sense of futility, and disconnection from God. But responding to Haggai's call to revival brought refreshing change.

Haggai 1:1-15
and Revelation 3:14-22

• What did God ask the Israelites to evaluate (Haggai 1:5-8)?

• What recommitments do you need to make with your own priorities?

thursday

How Can I Experience Revival Of My Faith?

The woman in today's verses had unsuccessfully looked for love and acceptance for years. Even though Jesus knew everything about the Samaritan woman's past and present, he fully accepted her. This acceptance led her finally to discover the Truth and gave her new hope for her future. The journey with Jesus begins with one step and then grows through continued encounters with God's loving acceptance that bring you back to your initial commitment to Jesus again and again.

John 4:1-42

• What seemed to revive the woman's spirit as she talked with Jesus?

• What about your first experience with Jesus encourages you to recommit to him on a daily basis?

Many who love God try to live each day under their own power, leaning on what they intellectually know about God. Nothing is more draining to mind, body, and spirit than trying to live out your faith through your own efforts. Spiritual renewal comes as a result of personally knowing God and giving control to the Holy Spirit who dwells in you as a follower of Jesus. The book of Acts describes powerful acts of the Spirit through those who submitted to the Spirit's control.

Acts 19:1-11

• What was the result of the Holy Spirit's presence in the lives of the believers? In Paul's life?

• In what ways are you willing to more fully submit to the Spirit's control?

Psalms is a book written by persons who experienced every emotion in life, including times of spiritual dryness and feeling disconnected from God. Even when you don't have words to describe your own situation, through the words of the psalmists it is possible to be honest with God, reconnect with God's grace and love, and be renewed in your relationship with Jesus.

Psalm 86:1-17

• List at least four reasons the psalmist was confident that God would answer his prayers.

• Of the promises David made in this psalm, which do you feel led to embrace for yourself?

the word on...
HUMILITY

Pride is defined in the dictionary as "a haughty attitude shown by people who believe, often unjustifiably, that they are better than others." While on Earth, Jesus would have had every reason to be proud of his sinless life and identity as God's Son. Yet Jesus took the opposite approach and assumed the humble attitude of a servant. Rather than a self-righteous attitude of superiority, Jesus modeled the humility of One sent to serve the needs of others.

Philippians 2:1-16

• According to Philippians 2:9-11, what was God's response to Jesus' demonstration of humility?

• Make a list of the characteristics of a humble attitude in believers, as listed in today's reading.

Jesus so wanted his followers to be known for demonstrating humility that he used his last night with the disciples to drive it home in a powerful way. In Jesus' day only the lowliest of servants would be assigned to wash the dusty feet of houseguests. But Jesus voluntarily assumed this menial task as a dramatic symbol of how God desires believers to humbly serve the needs of those around them. Rather than pridefully taking his place at the head of the table, Jesus took the task requiring the greatest humility.

John 13:1-16

• What did Jesus tell the disciples his motivation was for washing their feet?

• What act of service could you perform today that would give you the opportunity, like Jesus, to demonstrate humility?

Jesus' disciples, infected by the human tendency toward pride, were not shy about asking Jesus who was the "greatest" in God's kingdom. In their minds, their spiritual growth from spending time with Jesus was the path to heavenly power and position for themselves. But Jesus corrected his followers by explaining that the path from pride to humility, found through the surprising example of a child, is the true path to greatness.

Matthew 18:1-5 and 11:25-30

• According to Jesus, what about a child represents a humble attitude of heart and mind?

• What did Jesus say you could gain by giving him your burdens and learning from his "gentle and humble" heart?

wednesday

Both in Jesus' day and today, persons who love God can be tempted to measure themselves against those around them and feel smug about being more obedient, more faithful, or wiser. But Jesus told a stinging parable to illustrate God's low view of this kind of self-righteous pride. Jesus' message was that God values a repentant heart far more than the arrogance of a believer who looks down on others.

Luke 18:9-14 and Proverbs 22:4

• On what did the Pharisee focus in his prayer to God? What did the tax collector focus on?

• What self-righteous pride in yourself do you need God's help to deal with?

thursday

Practicing godly humility brings believers a completely different worldview. Jesus taught about this specifically in his Sermon on the Mount. The set of new mind-sets he described, called the Beatitudes, outlines how taking the path of humility step by step results in life-transforming spiritual growth. The Beatitudes represent the opposite approach from a secular, prideful way of living.

Matthew 5:1-12

• What steps did Jesus name as the path of humility, and what result did he predict for each?

• Which of the Beatitudes challenges you the most, and why?

Today's reading from Colossians is a beautiful description of what happens to relationships when humble attitudes are practiced. The harmony that is possible between believers is enabled only when each person honors, respects, and values others fully. Paul also wrote of another means God sometimes uses to help keep prideful believers, like Paul, humble: physical or emotional "reminders" of our own weaknesses and imperfections.

Colossians 3:12-17 and 2 Corinthians 12:5-10

• What qualities of humble, godly relationships are named in the Colossians passage?

• What "reminder" has God allowed you to have to keep a humble perspective of your constant need for God's grace?

One form of pride can show itself as a need for recognition that you are more important or more special than others. Motivated by desire for perceived power and authority in the eyes of those present, guests at a dinner party Jesus attended competed with one another to sit in the most privileged spots at the table. Jesus responded by giving a clear definition of how to avoid this type of pride and how to model humility instead. Jesus emphasized what kind of humble actions gain God's recognition.

Luke 14:7-14

• What were Jesus' instructions on how to avoid this type of pride?

• Evaluate your daily habits. How can you apply today's truths to practice more humility?

the word on...
GENEROSITY

How Generous Does God Expect Me To Be Financially?

Rather than looking at actual amounts given, God is more concerned with God-followers demonstrating a generous spirit and attitude toward others. Because God cares about people, you as God's follower are to be generous and openhanded with your financial resources to help "your brothers, sisters, the poor and needy" according to what you have.

Deuteronomy 15:1-11

• What does God promise those who operate out of a generous spirit and attitude (15:5-6)?

• With what are you most tempted to be tightfisted? What attitude shift could increase your generosity?

Mephibosheth was physically challenged, destitute, and powerless, but King David generously welcomed him into his house. Although not a relative, Mephibosheth lived in relationship with the king and was given full access to all the benefits of living in the king's household. Your demonstration of generous hospitality (with your home, time, possessions, food, and so forth) can give hope to those who feel unworthy and spiritually hopeless.

2 Samuel 9:1-13

• What did David provide for Mephibosheth (9:7-10)?

• Who has generously welcomed you into their lives and homes?

Today's verses give examples of two persons who generously demonstrated love for Jesus by giving sacrificially to him. A woman gave a special gift of expensive perfume and anointed Jesus before his death, and a little boy gave all his food to Jesus to use for the benefit of others. You show love to Jesus by honoring him and generously serving others.

Mark 14:3-9 and John 6:1-13

• In Mark 4, what was the disciples' objection to the woman's gift? How did Jesus defend her?

• Like the woman's perfume and the boy's lunch, what is the greatest thing you have to give? How will you offer it to Jesus for his use?

wednesday

Is Being Generous Just About My Money?

_____

A spiritually mature follower of Christ is characterized by generosity—not just with financial resources but in all areas of life. Those who claim to know and walk in obedience to Christ will liberally demonstrate Christ's character, which is summed up by the word *love*. Rather than an emotion, the biblical definition of *love* is deep concern resulting in right actions toward others. Today's Scripture gives a detailed description of what generous love is to look like and why it's to be the basis of everything you do.

1 Corinthians 13:1-13 and 1 Peter 1:22-23

• What qualities characterize the kind of generous love expected of a follower of Jesus?

• To whom would you point as a great example of being generous in loving others? Why?

thursday

How Does Generosity Relate To Faith?

_____

God-followers demonstrate an abundant, generous faith that sets the tone for their own lives and influences those around them for God. At the age of eighty, Daniel had lived a full, faith-filled life. He had gone through many experiences requiring him to stand firm and rely on God to provide. As an old man Daniel's enemies tried to use his faithfulness to God against him in an attempt to bring about Daniel's downfall. Generous faith in a trustworthy God is a winning combination.

Daniel 6:1-29

• What trap did the government officials set for Daniel? How did God work it out for him?

• In what situation have you had to depend (or are you depending) on God alone to come through?

Following Jesus means you have been "born again" into a new family—the family of believers. This new community has the responsibility to spur one another on to spiritual maturity. Each member needs to look for ways to generously encourage those around him or her to be everything they can be in Jesus. Encouragement takes many different forms, as described in today's verses. Paul went out of his way to encourage the Thessalonians, even when he was absent from them.

1 Thessalonians 2:17–3:13 and 5:9-28

• What specific actions did Paul encourage the Thessalonians to take in order to grow in spiritual maturity?

• Which of Paul's instructions is most encouraging to you?

You have choices in how you approach other people, including the way you address them verbally. In your humanness, it may be tempting to use your words for criticism, gossip, or to attack another person verbally. But a generous spirit expresses words that build up, not destroy.

Proverbs 15:1-4, 15:7, and James 3:1-12

• From Proverbs 15, what are the results of speaking out of a generous spirit?

• When was the last time you regretted something you said?

the word on...
GRATITUDE

sunday *Why Should I Be Grateful To God?*

_____

_____

_____

_____

_____

_____

_____

_____

_____

_____

_____

_____

Learning to recognize and appreciate the great love and care that God has for you will transform your life in miraculous ways. The Psalms describe very specifically the awesome and loving nature of God toward humanity. When you begin to focus on the full impact of God's personal all-encompassing love for you, a natural response is to begin to live a life of gratitude. Those who comprehend God's care and love for them praise and thank God daily.

Psalms 92 and 146

• Write down the incredible attributes and actions of God that the psalmist mentions. For which are you most grateful?

• For what are you most thankful to God today?

When you focus on the fact that God is ultimately the great provider, your appreciative and grateful relationship with God will deepen and mature. But in the day-to-day busyness of schedules, how easy it is to forget who it is that brings blessings and substance into your life! When that happens, soon you begin to take credit for all that you possess. And as you lose sight of God more and more, your focus changes to pursuing and worshiping things instead of the God who provides them.

Deuteronomy 8:1-20

• According to this passage, why did God allow times of both prosperity and scarcity in the lives of the Israelites?

• Is it easy for you to forget God as the great Provider when things are going well in your life? How can you make sure to remind yourself of that fact daily?

One major temptation you face in life is being envious of your friends, family, neighbors, and others you know because of the things that they possess and the life they seem to lead. Whether it's money, cars, houses, jobs, families, health, or other possessions, it's easy to want and desire what you don't have. However, Scripture is very clear that being envious is not only unwise and sinful but also can rob you of the life and peaceful sense of gratitude God wants for you.

James 3:13-18 and Psalm 73

• How do these passages describe the disorder and destruction that envy can bring you?

• Of whom or what do you struggle with being envious? For what can you be grateful instead?

wednesday · *How Do I Get Past Being Envious Of Others?*

_____

_____

_____

_____

_____

_____

_____

_____

_____

_____

_____

Envy of others not only robs you of life, it also keeps you from accomplishing the purposes God created you to fulfill. However, when you keep your eyes on God and gratefully live out the purpose for which you were created, like John the Baptist, you too can say that "the joy is mine, and [my work] is now complete."

John 3:22-36

• How did John the Baptist keep from being envious of Jesus' growing ministry while his ministry declined? Why was he joyful about Jesus' ministry?

• How can serving others keep you grateful for God's blessings, rather than envious for what you don't have?

thursday · *Where Does Gratitude Begin?*

_____

_____

_____

_____

_____

_____

_____

_____

_____

_____

_____

Gratitude must actually first take root in your heart. When you realize the enormity of your failures and sin versus the magnitude of God's love and grace for you through the sacrifice of Jesus Christ, it becomes easy to be deeply grateful at the heart level. Christ's indescribable love and forgiveness offer you new life and peace!

Luke 7:36-50

• The woman loved Jesus more than the Pharisee who invited Jesus to dinner did. Why? How did she show her gratitude?

• How do you show your love and gratitude to Jesus for forgiving you and giving you new life?

Gratitude definitely shows itself in your outward actions. By giving, you show both honor to God, who gives generously to you, and love for others, by sharing what you have been given. A lifestyle of grateful giving keeps you focused on God's abundance, not on what you have or don't have.

2 Corinthians 9:6-15 and Psalm 37:22-26

• Why does God bless you with abundance? How does giving show thanks to God?

• When you give offerings to God, the church, or directly to those in need, do you give out of gratitude, obligation, or guilt?

True gratitude means being thankful for what God gives you and content in any and every situation God places you. You can only be content, however, if you continually trust and rely on Christ, who will be faithful in meeting your needs. Contentment and peace are by-products of recognizing and appreciating who made you and who continually strengthens you with Christ's power and love.

Philippians 4:10-13, Hebrews 13:5-6, and 1 Timothy 6:3-10

• In Philippians 4, what does Paul say is the secret to being content?

• Are you content with what you have in life? Why or why not?

the word on...
FORGIVENESS

sunday — *What Did Jesus Teach About Forgiveness?*

_____
_____
_____
_____
_____
_____
_____
_____
_____
_____
_____
_____
_____

The topic of forgiveness is so important that Jesus included it in the Lord's Prayer, the prayer he taught his disciples. And after he taught them to pray, he explained further about the consequence of not forgiving others. According to Jesus, God's forgiveness for you is operative only to the extent that it flows through you out to others. If you refuse to forgive others, God's forgiveness for you is short-circuited. Individuals who are judgmental and critical of others are usually harboring grudges and refusing to forgive, unable to embrace God's forgiveness themselves.

Matthew 6:5-15

• Look at Matthew 6:12 and explain this part of the Lord's Prayer in your own words.

• Reread Matthew 6:14-15. What grudges are you holding on to? Is there someone you need to forgive?

All forgiveness has its beginnings in the very nature and character of God. Without your own experience of receiving forgiveness from God you can never begin to forgive others who have mistreated you or caused you pain. Not only does God forgive you of your sin and rebellion, God doesn't punish you as you really deserve. God also shows you love and compassion, and continually seeks an intimate relationship with you. This is what you are called to pass on to others.

Psalm 103

• Which statement in this psalm about God comforts you the most?

• What are some things for which you need to ask God's forgiveness?

It is easy to forget God's forgiving mercy toward you when others have hurt you. However, when you stack up all your own sins alongside the (often) minor offenses of others, there is usually no comparison. You have had such a great debt forgiven by God that, in gratitude and obligation, you are called to seek to forgive your brothers and sisters when they wrong you.

Matthew 18:21-35 and Luke 17:1-5

• What is the monetary comparison between the debt the servant owed the king and the debt he was owed by a fellow servant?

• Who has hurt you recently and needs to hear a forgiving word from you?

wednesday

_____

_____

_____

_____

_____

_____

_____

_____

_____

_____

_____

_____

Harboring unforgiveness can lead you down a very destructive path. Refusing to forgive leads to anger, and anger leads to resentment. When you let these emotions persist you are prone to do evil yourself. Forgiving others is the key to releasing potentially destructive feelings and avoiding destructive actions. Continually be on guard to walk in forgiving grace instead of anger or revenge.

Genesis 4:1-12 and Psalm 37:1-9

• What are consequences of anger and refusal to forgive listed in these passages? What happened to Cain?

• Describe a time you lashed out in anger instead of offering forgiveness. What would you do differently now?

thursday

_____

_____

_____

_____

_____

_____

_____

_____

_____

_____

_____

Nothing causes division among Christians more than unforgiveness and resentment. In the same manner, nothing is a greater witness to the world around you of the power of God than loving others through the pain of offense and wrongdoing. By forgiving others you not only maintain your unity and fellowship but also become an example of God's great forgiveness found in Jesus Christ.

Hebrews 12:14-15, 2 Corinthians 2:5-11, and 1 Peter 3:8-12

• According to these passages, how specifically are we to treat one another in the body of Christ?

• Have you ever repaid a blessing to someone who wronged you? What happened?

It is definitely easier to forgive someone who is truly sorry and asks for your forgiveness than someone who mistreats you and is unapologetic. Joseph finally had the opportunity, power, and justification to do much harm to his brothers and family, but he chose to forgive them for God's greater purpose. If you, too, will continually trust in God and believe that God can use anything for good—including sins committed against you—God will use your wounds for greater good as well.

Genesis 45:1-14 and Psalm 4

• In Genesis 45:5-8, how does Joseph commend God instead of condemn his brothers for selling him into Egypt?

• In what trial or hurt do you need to allow God to work for good?

While on Earth, Jesus taught about the importance of forgiveness and reconciliation, of loving your enemies and praying for those who persecute you. And in his death on the cross he modeled this for us all. Forgiveness is the path to living as children of our Father in heaven, instruments of godly reconciliation.

Matthew 5:21-24, 43-48, and Luke 23:26-43

• How did Jesus' forgiveness influence one of the thieves being crucified next to him?

• What do you see as the most important point Jesus made in the Matthew passage?

the word on...
PURITY

sunday *How Can I Keep Myself Pure Before God?*

_____

_____

_____

_____

_____

_____

_____

_____

_____

_____

_____

According to the Bible, your morality is often tested through the sexual part of your life. The Bible is not negative about sex—sex is God's idea, after all! Rather, God guides us to have sex exclusively within marriage for our protection and health—physically, spiritually, and emotionally. By living according to God's word, you can keep your way pure and experience this gift as God intended.

Psalm 119:1-16
and Proverbs 5:1-23

• According to Psalm 119:2 and 10, what is critical to keeping your way pure?

• From what source did you get your primary understanding of sex? What from today's Scripture could alter your viewpoint?

Jesus addressed, head-on, those who hypocritically attempted to appear "righteous" on the outside. He spoke of the need for change—not just of outside behavior, but of the inside thoughts and motivations that drive what you do. Jesus cannot be fooled or impressed; he knows that inside of every human lurk dark thoughts, attitudes, and motivations that can eventually tempt one to act inappropriately, unless God is allowed to deal with them.

Matthew 5:2-30 and James 1:12-18

• What is the cause of temptation, as named in James 1:14-15? What is its result?

• What sin are you currently dealing with internally that Jesus would tell you to "gouge out," "lose," or "cut off and throw away"?

King David is one of the Bible's heroes, yet even he struggled to maintain godly purity. By not being about his God-given responsibilities as commander-in-chief, he made himself vulnerable to sexual temptation. And his choices caused one act of disobedience to escalate into a domino effect of other sins in an attempt to cover the original wrongdoing. But David is not only an example of what not to do; he is also a model of the power of forgiveness in a personal relationship with God. David wrote Psalm 51 as a confession to God following his experience with Bathsheba.

2 Samuel 11:1-27 and Psalm 51

• Which four of the Ten Commandments (Exodus 20:1-17) did David break? What could David have done to prevent his string of sins from starting in the first place?

• When have you experienced the love and mercy of God like David described in Psalm 51?

wednesday

_____
_____
_____
_____
_____
_____
_____
_____
_____
_____
_____
_____

A pure heart is an undivided heart. As a resident of the world, you may have picked up its pattern and now have to commit yourself to following Jesus fully and letting God gradually, through God's grace and power, remold you to be like Jesus. This will probably mean giving up some familiar impure activities to avoid falling back into the pattern of the world. The habitual pattern of disobedience and removal of sin will gradually fade away as you let God live a holy life through you.

Matthew 5:8, 1 John 2:1-17, 2:28-29, and 3:1-10

• List reasons John gave for the importance of having your heart purely focused on God.

• As you grow older are certain sinful desires in your life harder or easier to submit to God?

thursday

_____
_____
_____
_____
_____
_____
_____
_____
_____
_____
_____
_____

The city of Corinth had a reputation throughout the first-century world as a center of pagan worship, extreme wealth, and excessive behavior, including sexual worship practices with temple prostitutes. Paul had to teach new Christians in Corinth the difference between the "everything is permissible" mind-set of the Corinthian culture and a lifestyle that honors a holy God. Sexual immorality dishonors God by violating the relationship between a person and the Spirit of Christ who dwells within.

1 Corinthians 6:12-20 and 7:1-7

• Whereas Paul was adamant in his condemnation of sexual promiscuity, what is his attitude toward the sexual relationship within marriage?

• Are you honoring God within your particular marital status?

The Gentiles were people of non-Jewish tradition. They were not guided by the Old Testament Law, let alone by a personal relationship with God. Their life patterns showed insensitivity to others, an indulgence in sensual pleasures, and a tendency to see others as objects to use for their own benefit. Paul urged Christ followers to reject that lifestyle and instead be imitators of God in how they treated one another, including in their sexual relationships.

Ephesians 4:17-24 and 5:1-16

• How can you "find out what pleases the Lord"?

• What ways can you identify within yourself that confirm you are putting off your old self and putting on the new?

Two natures are at war within every follower of Christ. The old nature, which wants to look out for number one and use other people to achieve its goals, is face-to-face with the Holy Spirit, who wants to empower you to live and love like Jesus. You will inevitably partner with one or the other—the choice is yours.

Romans 13:8-14
and Galatians 5:16-26

• According to Paul, what are we to do with our sinful nature (Romans 13:14 and Galatians 5:24)?

• What does it look like to keep in step with the Spirit? How can you do so better?

the word on...
GOD'S PROMISES

sunday *How Do I Begin Fully Living Out God's Promises?*

_____

_____

_____

_____

_____

_____

_____

_____

_____

_____

_____

_____

The Christian life is rooted in the wonderful grace of God, but that is just the first step. God has much more for you than making you alive again through Christ. You were created to live a full life of purpose, doing the good work God has prepared for you to do. The Bible, God's word, is filled with promises of how God desires to supernaturally provide resources to you through the power of the Holy Spirit.

Ephesians 2:1-10

• List some of the powerful promises of God offered to you in this passage.

• What kind of purposeful work is God placing in your heart to accomplish?

Sometimes you may feel discouraged and wonder if God actually desires to help you grow and succeed in faithfulness. Good news: God's love for you is far greater than you can understand or even imagine! And in that love you can have confident assurance that God is not only capable but also eager to help you live your life in all the fullness God intended. No matter what your past struggles or downfalls, God's word offers hope and promises for renewal and strength.

2 Corinthians 1:18-22 and 2 Peter 1:3-4

• According to 2 Corinthians 1, how do you know that you have and can live in the promises of God? What has God provided you to live out this godly life (2 Peter 1:3)?

• In what areas of your life do you trust God, and in what areas do you struggle with trusting God?

In order to continue living out the godly life of purpose and promise, you must always be on guard against temptation and sin. Since compromise and sin easily entangle followers of Jesus and can keep you from walking the path God has marked out for you, work to remain diligent in fighting against them. In today's reading, believers are not only warned about falling into temptation but also told how to stand up against the evil that wars against them.

1 Corinthians 10:1-13 and Hebrews 2:14-18

• From these passages, list the different ways God helps believers overcome temptation and evil.

• What are some of your weaknesses in terms of temptation and compromise? How can you do better at protecting yourself from these?

wednesday
What Is God's Promise When I'm Distressed Or Brokenhearted?

_____
_____
_____
_____
_____
_____
_____
_____
_____
_____
_____

Life is definitely difficult at times. It becomes very easy at those moments to forget all about the promises of God and stop living out the faithful life you are called to live, empowered by God's promises. Where is God when things go wrong and this life turns hard? In the readings today, you will get a better picture not only of God's amazing concern for you, but also how you are to respond in the tough moments of life.

Psalms 30 and 34:17-20

• In Psalm 30, what did David (the author) do when he found himself in the valleys of life? What was God's faithful response to David?

• Do you spend more or less time seeking God when challenges come? What promise of God from these passages do you need to stand on in the midst of trouble?

thursday
How Do I Know When I Am Going In The Right Direction?

_____
_____
_____
_____
_____
_____
_____
_____
_____
_____
_____
_____

Living a life of godly purpose and promise implies that you continually walk in the will and direction that God desires. Even though today you don't know God's entire will, God promises to provide what you need to walk in that right direction on a daily basis. Following God's guidance and promises means purposefully living in the light, both in public and in the Christian community. It is when you find yourself seeking isolation, secrecy, and darkness that you tend to be off track and in trouble with sin and compromise.

John 8:12, 12:34-36, and 1 Thessalonians 5:4-11

• In John 8:12, what does Jesus promise to those who follow him? What are all the things that walking in the light implies for our daily lives? What is implied by "darkness"?

• What are some of the ways you can purposefully stay in the light? How can you let other believers help you?

At times, guilt and shame from wrong things you've done may drive you away from the God who loves you. You can try to clean up your act on your own, and thus continue to fail. Instead, ask God's forgiveness and be filled again with the Spirit's power for supernatural living. Be assured that just as earthly parents seek to love and guide their children no matter what, God will also never let you go—you are a beloved child and an heir to the Kingdom.

John 10:22-30 and Hebrews 13:5-6

• What comfort do you receive in knowing that nothing can ever snatch you away from the hand of Jesus Christ? How does knowing this help you when you struggle in your Christian walk?

• Is going directly to God in times of failure and sin easy or difficult for you to do?

Walking the life of God's promises and purpose does not mean that you will never face trials. In fact, Jesus' disciple Peter wrote that everyone who wants to lead a godly life in Christ Jesus will be persecuted. Remember always that you have not only a God who promises protection but also a God who truly cares for all of your anxieties. God's goal is not to save you from suffering but to make you strong so that through all things you may continue to love and serve others in need.

1 Peter 5:6-11 and Psalm 91:1-16

• What are God's promises to you in 1 Peter 5:6-11? What does God promise in Psalm 91:14-16 when it comes to being in trouble?

• What cares do you need to give God today?

the word on...
MODERATION

What Happens When Satisfying My Appetite Becomes The Driving Force In My Life?

In Old Testament culture the oldest son was awarded the "birthright," or an extra portion of the father's inheritance. In the case of Jacob and Esau, the birthright was the covenant of God as well as material possessions. Esau, Isaac's elder son, was a man driven by his appetite, and he sold his birthright for a pot of stew. The temporary satisfaction of his physical desire for food was a higher priority than an ongoing relationship with God.

Genesis 25:19-34
and Hebrews 12:16-17

• How did Esau's actions fulfill the prophecy concerning him and his brother in Genesis 25:23?

• Have you ever made a hasty decision based on physical drives that resulted in long-lasting consequences? What happened?

It will always be tempting to run with your physical appetites for eating and drinking. Physical desires are strong, and you can allow them to be the deciding factor in your actions. When you practice overindulgence and excess in these areas, you are practicing what the Bible calls "gluttony." Your decisions on how to handle yourself are based on your understanding of who you are in Christ and how much respect you have for yourself, the work of God's hands.

Isaiah 5:11-12
and 1 Corinthians 9:24-27

• To what or whom is each of the runners in Isaiah 5:11 and 1 Corinthians 9:24 running? What motivates each runner?

• What positive decisions about handling your physical appetites will you make for today?

_____
_____
_____
_____
_____
_____
_____
_____
_____
_____
_____

After crossing the Red Sea from Egypt, the Israelites found themselves in a desert void of food and water. For forty years God provided a daily supply of water, quail, and manna (bread) to meet their nutritional needs. Most of the Israelites trusted God and depended on God's food supply to be there. But some of the people tried to hoard an excess of food, which spoiled overnight. Overindulging or hoarding reflects dependence on self rather than God in meeting your physical, emotional, and spiritual needs.

Exodus 16:9-30
and Psalm 78:15-32

• What did Moses promise the people (Exodus 16:11)? What instruction did he give them (Exodus 16:19)? Why?

• In what scenarios are you most likely to overindulge your appetites?

_____
_____
_____
_____
_____
_____
_____
_____
_____
_____

wednesday

_____

_____

_____

_____

_____

_____

_____

_____

_____

_____

Paul was experienced in dealing with excess. Before knowing Christ he sought meaning through an insatiable appetite not for food but for overachievement and recognition. After coming into a relationship with Christ, Paul no longer put confidence in the flesh (his own abilities, significance, and habits) but was progressively learning to depend on the resurrection power of Christ in his life.

Philippians 3:3-21

• How does Paul describe those who put confidence in the flesh rather than in Christ (3:18-19)?

• What is taking the place of Jesus in your life and needs to die so you can know "the power of his resurrection" instead?

thursday

_____

_____

_____

_____

_____

_____

_____

_____

_____

_____

Excessive behavior can be a result of attempts to fill the spiritual void only God can fill. Although you may try to fill the spiritual void with physical substitutes, they cannot meet your spiritual needs. If you don't look to the Source who can really fulfill your needs, your behavior can become repetitive and extreme (gluttony), and your anxiety level will soar. In today's verses, Jesus addressed the issue of substituting food and drink for the presence of God and challenged his followers to totally abandon themselves to God's care.

Matthew 6:25-34
and Proverbs 21:20

• According to Matthew 6, what is the cause of anxiety and worry? What assurance does God give?

• What gives you the greatest security—material things and physical satisfaction, or your relationship with God?

Jesus counseled his followers to be about the right things, always living in expectancy of his promised return to Earth. You are not to get sidetracked by excessive behaviors such as drinking or eating. Paul also advised Jesus' followers to be sharp and alert, maintaining daily discipline in their relationship with Jesus in order to be prepared to face God, unhindered by the effects of excessive behavior.

1 Thessalonians 5:1-8
and Luke 21:29-38

• What did Jesus (Luke 21:34-36) and Paul (1 Thessalonians 5:6-8) warn followers to avoid?

• What is your biggest stumbling block when it comes to discipline?

Scripture gives insight into ways you can help yourself in your struggles with your appetite. Don't hang out with people who practice the very things that cause you to fall. Surround yourself with people who will support you and hold you accountable in your areas of struggle. Depend moment by moment on Jesus, who has placed his divine power within you and gives you everything you need for health and a God-honoring life.

Proverbs 23:19-21
and 2 Peter 1:3-11

• From 2 Peter 1:3-4, what is God's part in helping you live a God-honoring life? From verses 5-9, what is your part?

• Do those closest to you help or hinder your commitment to control your appetites and live a God-honoring life?

the word on...
DISCIPLINE

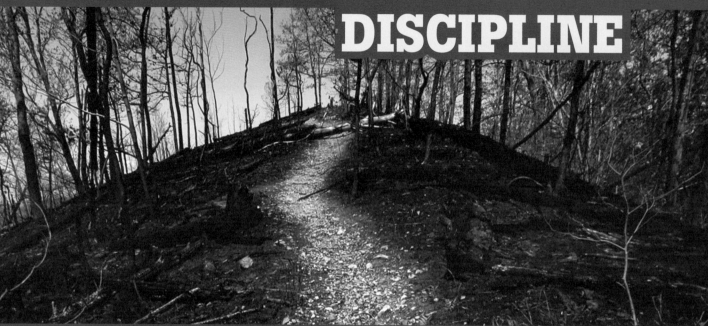

sunday   *Why Is Living A Disciplined Life Important?*

Both physical and spiritual discipline are essential in the daily life of a believer. Sometimes Christians don't equate laziness and the lack of physical discipline with spiritual consequences. But as you learn this week about discipline in both the spiritual and physical aspect, you will see how important each is to life transformation. Just as you might go into disciplined physical training to lose weight, get in shape, or even to run a marathon, you also need to train for spiritual victory.

1 Corinthians 9:24-27
and 1 Timothy 4:7-16

• Write down the words Paul uses in both of these passages to describe his view of discipline and spiritual work.

• Have you ever trained yourself to accomplish a certain goal? What could be applied from that experience to help you in your spiritual discipline?

Just as there are physical consequences for being lazy or not working hard, there is also a harmful spiritual dimension to idleness. As leaders, both Solomon and Paul were very aware of the example they set for their people in this way. And they also gave strong warning to those who aren't disciplined in life. Keep in mind, as you read today's passages, that God not only ordained work to be a blessing to us but also urged us never to tire of doing what is right and good.

Proverbs 10:4, 13:4, 14:23, 20:4, and 2 Thessalonians 3:6-15

• Compare and write down the different descriptions and conclusions for each of the proverbs.

• In what behaviors do you need to be more diligent?

Even though you can't always see the long-term effect of living a diligent and disciplined lifestyle on a daily basis, Scripture is clear that it will help you survive tough times and allow you to live free. Discipline does take work and definitely isn't the easy path. But with consistency and steadfast effort, you will be able to keep yourself on the right path and be in a position to be used by God for God's greater purposes.

Proverbs 6:1-11 and Luke 6:46-49

• What is the description of the ant and its work ethic? What did Jesus say is needed to build a solid and firm life foundation?

• What is one thing you need to start doing to become a disciplined disciple of Jesus?

wednesday *Does God Honor Persistent Discipline In Prayer?*

_____

_____

_____

_____

_____

_____

_____

_____

_____

_____

Sometimes you can become lazy or halfhearted about bringing to God your own prayer requests, as well as those on behalf of others. But Jesus clearly taught that believers needed to be disciplined in their approach to God by continually turning to God in prayer. It's not that God is slow to hear or respond to your requests. God wants to teach you to rely on the One who truly knows what's best for your life.

Luke 11:5-13 and 18:1-8

• Why did both the neighbor and judge give in to the requests put upon them? How does this compare to God, who truly loves and desires to take care of your needs?

• What personal request or need of a friend might necessitate more persistent prayer to God from you?

thursday *How Does Discipline Affect My Service For Jesus Christ?*

_____

_____

_____

_____

_____

_____

_____

_____

_____

_____

God created you for mission and a purpose that comes directly from Jesus Christ; in gratitude you are called to do all you can to fulfill that work. God does expect you to be a faithful, diligent worker in serving out the mission of Jesus. In order to do the work of Christ you must be disciplined and not become lethargic or apathetic. Otherwise, you will dishonor God's call.

Matthew 25:14-30

• Write down the words that the master used to describe those who pleased him versus the one who displeased him. What was the outcome for each servant?

• Are you afraid (like the third servant) or ready (like the other two) to go "at once" and serve God's work diligently? Explain.

It is easy to get distracted and off-track from living a focused and disciplined Christian life. The witness and example of others can keep you heading in the right direction. Whether it's the example of Christians currently around you now, or those who have lived before you, many who continually cheer you on surround you. Not only that, you also have Christ himself giving you daily direction, power, guidance, and strength.

Hebrews 12:1-13

• From the first three verses, write down all the things that encourage you (or could hinder you) in continuing a disciplined Christian life.

• Who are among your "cloud of witnesses" and help you run your Christian race? Whom can you cheer on yourself?

What Is The Ultimate Goal Of A Disciplined Christian Life? **saturday**

Even though discipline has many values for both the physical and spiritual aspects of life, the goal of discipline is to keep you pressing forward to grasp all that Christ would have for your life. Discipline keeps your eyes focused on the present as well as the future so that you can completely maximize this life that God has called you to live.

Philippians 3:12–4:1

• How did Paul, the author of today's reading, stay disciplined and focused as he continued in his walk with Christ?

• What do you honestly need to leave behind in your effort to strive forward in Christ? Write a prayer, releasing it now.

the word on...
TRUST

sunday

What Example Did Jesus Give Of Trusting God Fully?

_____

_____

_____

_____

_____

_____

_____

_____

_____

_____

_____

_____

Jesus taught his disciples about living in trust and dependence on God alone by contrasting the religious leaders of his day with a widow living in poverty. The religious leaders lived for the accolades of people and made their wealth at the expense of the powerless. They donated to God but relied on themselves and their financial resources. The poor widow quietly gave all she had, trusting that God alone would provide what she needed.

Mark 12:38-43

• How did the widow actually give more than all the others, even though she was poor (Mark 12:43)?

• Are you torn between serving two masters (God and money)? What needs to change?

Throughout Scripture, a tight correlation is described between knowing God intimately and trusting God completely. In Proverbs 3:6, "in all your ways acknowledge [God]" is best translated "in all your ways know God." As you develop your relationship with God in every part of life, including your finances, you will increasingly trust and live out God's wisdom, priorities, and power.

Proverbs 3:1-15

• What are you commanded to do in order to gain God's wisdom and guidance?

• How does the directive to honor God with the "first fruits" (the first 10 percent) of your finances challenge you (3:9)?

Jesus first encountered Simon Peter, James, and John—his future disciples—at a time of their discouragement. Regardless of their efforts, they could not capture the resources they needed. When you face discouragement in your finances, career, or family life, Jesus calls you to come deeper into your relationship with him, trust his direction, and see what he will do in your life situation.

Luke 5:1-11

• Why did the three disciples leave everything behind and follow Jesus?

• Have you been struggling in any way to produce results on your own and need to surrender to Jesus instead?

wednesday

_____

_____

_____

_____

_____

_____

_____

_____

_____

_____

_____

One of the hot topics in biblical times as well as today is the possession and use of money. Paul taught that inner contentment results from a genuine relationship with God and a healthy detachment from material things. Although all followers of Christ are called to "do good" and "be rich in good deeds," those who are blessed with material wealth have an even greater responsibility to manage their resources for God's glory and for the benefit of others.

1 Timothy 6:6-21

• Why are you to not put your hope and trust in wealth? What are you to put your hope in instead?

• Look at 1 Timothy 6:10-11. What step do you need to take next to flee the temptation of money, pursue godliness in a deeper way, or both?

thursday

_____

_____

_____

_____

_____

_____

_____

_____

_____

_____

_____

Learning to trust God sometimes means stepping out of your comfort zone, where you feel in control and capable of handling your life situation, and simply trusting God to uphold you. It may be risky for you to step out of your comfort zone and give according to biblical standards, but only as you act in faith will you have the opportunity to see God's promise to meet your needs come true.

Matthew 14:22-33
and Luke 6:37-38

• What did Peter discover about Jesus when he stepped out of the safety of the boat?

• How specifically do you hear Jesus calling you to step out and trust him? Will you do it?

Financial management is often a blind spot in the mind and heart of a Jesus follower. As a result, what you believe and what you do with your finances may be two different things. Saying you trust God but relying on credit (rather than scaling back to live within your means) can bring the bondage and oppression of debt, rather than bringing honor and glory to God. God will help you navigate the minefield of your financial situation as you set your mind to living within what God has provided you, rather than following your own desires.

1 John 2:15-17 and Psalm 62

• The psalmist warned God's followers not to trust three things in 62:10. What are they?

• How do the psalmist's statements about God in 62:5-8 reflect your experience with God?

There is nothing so certain as the biblical affirmation of God's love for and good intentions toward you. God is on your side! When you are asked to grow in your giving and serving, there need not be fear of what God asks you to do. As you "seek [God] with all your heart," you will find that your help in all things comes from the Lord, who watches over you day and night.

Jeremiah 29:11-14 and Psalm 121

• Summarize God's promises for you from today's Scriptures.

• When have you seen God's protection for you? Where do you need God's help now?

the word on...
RESOURCES

sunday
Can God Multiply My Resources When Surrendered In Faith?

_____

_____

_____

_____

_____

_____

_____

_____

_____

_____

_____

Elijah's experiences required the utmost faith in God. Destitute and hungry, Elijah was miraculously fed by ravens. When Elijah's water supply ran out, God led him to a foreign country where he had to depend on the good intentions of a starving, poverty-stricken widow to survive. This widow put her faith in what the "LORD, the God of Israel" said and offered all her resources for God to multiply to meet the needs of Elijah and her family. God multiplies whatever you have as you step out and risk entrusting those resources to God.

1 Kings 17:1-15

• What did Elijah tell the widow to do to combat her fears? What was the result?

• Identify a time when God stretched your resources to meet your needs and the needs of others. What happened?

When God calls you to a specific work, God will create a passion for that work within you and will give you the resources you need to fulfill God's call. After centuries of waiting, the Israelites in Babylonian exile longed to return to their homeland in Palestine; God lit a fire within Ezra to lead the movement back to Jerusalem. Ezra gathered the people and the resources that the Persian king and others had given them. He followed through and acted to complete the rebuilding of the temple in Jerusalem and to train the Israelite people to be a community that would faithfully serve God.

Ezra 1:1-11

• How did God provide the needed resources for the people to return to Jerusalem and rebuild the temple?

• How are you using the financial and spiritual resources God has given you to serve God?

There is not just one way to use your resources to show love for Jesus. Today's Scripture passage gives an example of love shown for Jesus, expressed through personal care. It may be tempting to criticize others, as some of the disciples did, for showing love in a different manner than you would. But Jesus understood the love and honor this woman generously expressed by sacrificially offering her precious resource.

Mark 14:3-9

• Why were the disciples upset with the woman's gift to Jesus? What would they have done instead?

• How could you use your personal resources to show unique and generous care in the name of Jesus to someone close to you?

wednesday
What Happens If I Claim Ownership Of God's Resources For Myself?

_____

_____

_____

_____

_____

_____

_____

_____

_____

_____

A popular song speaks of "giving you the best that I've got." That is exactly what Abel did in offering the best of his flocks to God. The attitude of his brother Cain was totally different, shown by his offering of "some" (a lesser quality and quantity) of his produce, rather than an animal that could be sacrificed on the altar. An underlying attitude of resentment toward God and claiming ownership of God's resources for yourself will result in giving God less than your best and will undercut your relationship with God and others.

Genesis 4:1-7 and Hebrews 11:4

• What was Cain's reaction to God's confrontation? What was the result?

• Do you ever struggle with giving up ownership of the resources God has given you?

thursday
How Are God's Resources To Be Used Within The Church?

_____

_____

_____

_____

_____

_____

_____

_____

_____

_____

_____

Believers in the New Testament church knew about stepping out in faith. They lived in a time of intense persecution and banded together to make sure everyone in the community was cared for and all needs were met. Individuals did not hoard their personal resources, but instead recognized them as gifts from God for the entire community. They serve as a dynamic example of what happens when the community of Christ uses the resources of God for the benefit of all.

Acts 2:42-47

• List the outcomes within the New Testament church as a result of believers pooling their resources and boldly living for Jesus.

• What could you personally model to your network of Christian friends as encouragement to be more like the New Testament community?

In What Ways Has God Equipped And Provided Resources For Me?

friday

Moses is one of the heroes of faith, but even he had to figure out how God had equipped him to serve. God's lesson to Moses: look at what is right in your hand. God's resources are not invisible. You just need to recognize and develop them. Moses obeyed God in some very risky situations but always had what he needed in order to do what God called him to do. Whether it's your finances, family, occupation, or ministry, look at what is already "in your hand" and use it to serve God fully.

Exodus 3:14–4:17

• What did Moses fear would happen if he did what God asked him to do? What were God's responses to him?

• What excuses hold you back from fully using the resources God has given you and doing what God has asked of you?

Why Are God's Followers Called To "Excel" In Sharing The Resources God Has Provided?

saturday

Paul used the example of the Macedonian churches to encourage other Christian believers to give financial support to those in need. Even when they were struggling financially themselves, the Macedonians joyfully gave. The Macedonians' example of giving reflected how Jesus sacrificially gave his life for all of humanity, and it fueled their trust that God would provide for and through them as they also sacrificially gave to others.

2 Corinthians 8:1-15

• List principles of giving that you observe in this passage.

• How does your giving reflect the example of Jesus' giving?

the word on...
CHOICES

sunday *Is My Spiritual Future Determined By My Own Choices?*

_____
_____
_____
_____
_____
_____
_____
_____
_____
_____
_____
_____
_____
_____

God has blessed you with the freedom of choice. How you choose to invest your life, your time, and especially your resources every day will determine whether you are investing in an earthly "portfolio" of material gain, or an eternal "portfolio" of treasure that will last. In God's eyes, how you choose to invest what you have on behalf of others demonstrates your faithfulness to Christ. In fact, Jesus taught that the measure of generosity you use to give of your resources influences how you will experience God's blessings.

Luke 6:30-38

• What behavior toward others does Jesus want us to choose when sharing money and resources?

• Up to now, have the choices you've made with your money and resources demonstrated Jesus' teachings? What needs to change?

While on Earth, Jesus taught his followers many times about choosing a path of trust in God's provision rather than hoarding possessions and money. Today's reading about a rich man building bigger barns in order to keep as much as possible for himself represents the opposite of the choice of faith Jesus recommended. In fact, Jesus taught of the simple abundance God will provide when your treasure is found in a life of faithfulness, rather than in fear of sharing your money.

Luke 12:13-34

• What is the point Jesus tried to make about greed versus faith?

• What message of assurance does this Scripture provide regarding your worry and fear about choosing to give?

Over and over the Bible describes the extravagant riches and resources of God, Creator of all heaven and Earth. How awe-inspiring to think that as you choose to demonstrate obedience to Christ, all your needs will be abundantly supplied through God's limitless provision. All too often believers live with a "scarcity" mentality, worrying that God somehow will not provide adequately for what is needed. But God is a God of plenty, and God has the supernatural power to provide you a new life, a new perspective, and a new hope.

Psalm 40

• According to this Psalm, what is God capable of providing? What does God want from you?

• How does knowing that God's resources are limitless affect your spiritual ability to choose to trust that your every need will be met?

wednesday

What Is The Relationship Between What I Believe And What I Choose?

God considers faithful choices to be ones that are backed up by corresponding actions. It is easy to promise God that you will be a wise steward of the money with which you've been blessed—but that promise means nothing if it's not demonstrated by how you take the firm step of faith to make good on it. Even if making a faithful choice with your resources is difficult at first, God is pleased with those who follow through and demonstrate their faith through their actions.

Matthew 21:28-32
and James 2:14-26

• What examples of faith demonstrated by action did James give?

• From Jesus' parable, which son have you most been like with the choices you've made regarding your resources? How is God speaking to you through this parable?

thursday

I've Made Poor Choices—Is It Too Late To Change?

With God, it's never too late to become obedient in your financial choices—starting today. God does not compare you to other believers who have handled their resources and money more wisely for longer than you have. Instead, God rejoices and rewards you according to your willingness to practice healthy stewardship of what you have right now. Your heavenly Master desires you to begin working now on investments that enhance your eternal portfolio and will be equally pleased with all who've been faithful when the day is done.

Matthew 20:1-16

• Why were the longest-working servants judgmental of their newest coworkers? What was the Master's reaction?

• What "time" are you getting started with choices to live faithfully for God—early, midway, or late in life? According to this parable, what is God's perspective?

Jesus demonstrated that radical followers are not to be like the Pharisees, the legalistic religious leaders of his day. The Pharisees kept their distance from broken, sinful people and believed favor with God was earned through ritualistic fasting and other legalistic religious practices. Jesus, however, modeled a lifestyle of love and compassion for those who desperately needed healing and transformation. He used the analogy of needing new wineskins to contain new wine to explain how a new life in Christ cannot also accommodate "old wine" or old, sinful choices.

Mark 2:13-22

• What did Jesus identify as his mission (Mark 2:17)?

• Through Christ you have received a new life or "new wineskin." What new choices do you need to make to replace old behaviors that aren't compatible with a faith-filled lifestyle?

Jesus used the example of a tiny mustard seed to emphasize how even the smallest choice made in faith will yield spiritual results far beyond what you can imagine. Honoring God with every one of your choices in all areas of your life—physically, relationally, emotionally, and financially—will "leaven" your entire life on behalf of God's ideal plans for you. Some believers think that choosing to be faithful to God will yield extra "bonus points" of favor. But Jesus taught that faithful choices are all part of what is expected of a sold-out servant of Christ.

Luke 17:5-10 and Matthew 13:31-34

• In Luke 17, his disciples asked Jesus to "increase their faith." What did Jesus mean by his response to their question?

• What is one new choice you have made as a believer that, like a mustard seed, started small and has grown to have results beyond what you expected?

the word on...
THANKFULNESS

sunday *How Do I Create An Attitude Of Thankfulness?*

_____

_____

_____

_____

_____

_____

_____

_____

_____

_____

_____

_____

_____

In becoming a genuinely thankful person, you must understand that thankfulness has its roots in the greatness and wonder of God. You may often be prone to ignore the majesty of God, living in your own world and the bustle of day-to-day activity. The first step in cultivating an attitude of thankfulness is remembering that God is an awesome and powerful God who not only created you but also created all things. It is in God that you, along with everyone and everything in creation, have your being and purpose.

Psalm 147:1-11
and Revelation 7:9-17

• List words used in these passages that describe God.

• Which of these words speak to you most about God's greatness, and why?

Just as you may often fail to acknowledge God's power and magnificence, you may also forget that all provision comes from God as well. In truly being thankful, make sure you recognize and acknowledge God's goodness to you and the many blessings you enjoy. This will help you remember that God is the One actually in control. God loves to bless you, and an attitude of thankfulness will keep you from becoming ungrateful or selfish as you continually rely on God for all things.

James 1:16-18 and Psalm 145:1-21

• From Psalm 145, list blessings that God provides you.

• Are you usually a thankful person, indifferent, or ungrateful when it comes to your blessings?

As a follower of Jesus, you have much for which to be thankful, but nothing is greater than your salvation and redemption from sin. And yet God promises even more than that. Not only are you saved by God's grace, you also are promised the Holy Spirit to guide you to victory over sin and to eternal life with Christ. To have such a great hope now and for the future is an overwhelming reason to be thankful in whatever circumstances you find yourself—good or bad.

Ephesians 2:1-10 and 1 Corinthians 15:50-58

• According to Ephesians 2, why does God show you so much mercy (verses 4-5)?

• Look at 1 Corinthians 15:57. In what has Christ's power given you victory?

wednesday
How Can I Be Thankful Even In Tough Times?

_____
_____
_____
_____
_____
_____
_____
_____
_____
_____
_____
_____

It's easy to be thankful when you receive blessings from God and things are going well in your life. It is a bit tougher to be thankful in difficult times or when everything in your life is seemingly going wrong. However, even then you can practice thankfulness that God is in control and is already at work in your circumstances. There is light at the end of whatever tunnel you're traveling. Keep trusting, and keep your thankful attitude active.

Philippians 4:4-9
and Psalm 30:1-12

• According to these passages, what are the promises you have from God even in the midst of trouble?

• What is an anxious area in your life right now and how can you begin to release that to God in prayer?

thursday
How Does My Thankfulness Allow God To Continually Work In My Life?

_____
_____
_____
_____
_____
_____
_____
_____
_____
_____
_____
_____

You may recognize God at work in the difficult times of life, a realization that increases both your faith and thankfulness. In today's readings you'll find both Moses and Daniel facing difficult situations but never letting go of their gratitude and confidence that God was continually working in their situations. Just as God worked then, God works now in your circumstances. That gives you deep reason to be thankful and opens your life of faith to stretch and grow.

Exodus 14:13-31
and Daniel 2:14-24

• How did Moses and Daniel thank God for working on their behalf?

• Do these passages give you hope for your own difficult circumstances? Thank God ahead of time for God's provision.

It may seem at times that serving others is so "thankless" that God should be thanking you for helping those who are in need. But the Apostle Paul gives us a different outlook, and for good reason. Not only is serving the Lord's mission a great privilege, but you also find both spiritual meaning and purpose when you fulfill those tasks to which God calls you. Being the hands and feet of Jesus in the world is a privilege. Practice responding with humility and thanksgiving for that honor.

1 Timothy 1:12-17 and 2 Corinthians 2:12–3:6

• In 1 Timothy, how did Paul regard his own call to service and ministry of Jesus Christ?

• Are you involved in serving Christ in mission and ministry right now? Do you have an attitude of thankfulness?

Even if you have seasons of frustration or tragedy when you struggle to be thankful, at the heart of your life as a believer you can always celebrate and be thankful for God's unfailing love. David wrote in today's passages that those who have encountered this vast love of God cannot help experiencing awe and wonder. God loves you no matter who you are or what you have done—and it is in this love that you can always thankfully find life, peace, and joy.

Psalms 100:1-5 and 118:1-29

• How does David describe his thankfulness for God's unfailing love?

• Think of a time when you have experienced the great compassionate love of God in your life, and write a prayer of thankfulness.

the word on...
SELF-DENIAL

sunday

What Part Does Self-Denial Play In Fulfilling God's Call?

_____

_____

_____

_____

_____

_____

_____

_____

_____

_____

_____

_____

_____

Mary, the mother of Jesus, provides an inspiring biblical example of the power of saying yes to God and no to self. When told her life call involved a supernatural birth, she recognized the risk to her reputation and her life. According to Old Testament law, pregnancy while unmarried was punishable by stoning. And the security of her relationship with her fiancé, Joseph, was at stake. However, her faith in God was based in such utter trust that she could respond, "I am the Lord's servant. May it be to me as you have said."

Luke 1:26-56

• What was Mary's initial response to the angel's message? How did the angel answer her?

• In what challenging situation could you, like Mary, praise God anyway for the opportunity to be faithful?

Whereas the Christmas story in the Gospel of Luke concentrates on Mary's perspective, the account in Matthew presents this world-changing event through Joseph's experience. Like Mary, Joseph's life was turned upside down. By saying yes to God and repeatedly putting his personal life plans on hold, Joseph ensured that Jesus would be protected, live to adulthood, and fulfill his life mission of reconciling all of humanity to God. One person's faith-filled self-denial benefits many others.

Matthew 1:18-25 and 2:13-23

• How many times did Joseph do what God commanded him? With what results?

• When you sense God is asking you to act in obedience, how long does it normally take you to say yes and follow through?

James and John were two of Jesus' closest friends. They were with Jesus at every teaching opportunity, but even they did not understand Jesus' mission and the sacrifice it would require. The innate craving for power and the desire to self-promote have nothing to do with what Jesus is about. His followers must abandon the world's idea of authority as "lording it over" others, drink from Jesus' cup of self-denial, and be transformed into servants of all.

Mark 10:32-45

• How did Jesus live out this life-teaching that he gave to his disciples?

• Who to you is a great example of personal sacrifice and self-denial? Why?

wednesday

_____

_____

_____

_____

_____

_____

_____

_____

_____

_____

Once the disciples identified Jesus as the Christ (the Savior; the Anointed One of God), Jesus began to teach them about his mission. The ways of God may conflict with human ideas, and Jesus rebuked Peter for operating out of human wisdom rather than pursuing God's. At the cross, Jesus faced God's will for him, which required the ultimate self-denial. Every day Jesus' followers must make the decision to take up their crosses, deny their own desires and understanding, and choose God's will. As you take up your cross and follow, you grow stronger as a disciple of Christ and deeper in your relationship with him.

Mark 8:27-38

• According to Jesus in Mark 8:34, what three things are required to follow Jesus?

• Put Mark 8:35-38 in your own words. What needs to change in your life in order for this to fully be true of you?

thursday

_____

_____

_____

_____

_____

_____

_____

_____

_____

_____

Following Jesus is not the continuation of life as it has previously been, with the addition of Jesus' stamp of approval. There is a cost in following Jesus, and that cost involves change. Personal agendas, relationships, and understandings all are affected by the call to self-denial. Those wanting to follow Jesus must count the cost to see if they can go the distance with him.

Luke 14:25-35

• In verse 33, what is the cost of following Jesus? What does this mean in terms of family and personal agenda?

• How costly has it been for you to follow Jesus?

Following Jesus is about an intimate, personal relationship with God through Jesus. The rich young ruler confused this relationship with living according to an external standard. Jesus knows your heart and can quickly identify the one thing that would keep you from following him fully. It may be wealth, a relationship, bitterness, substance abuse, workaholism—or any number of things. Whatever the reason is for you, Jesus calls you to give up whatever is blocking your relationship with him: "Then come, follow me."

Luke 18:18-30

• Compare the response of the rich young ruler to Jesus' challenge with Peter's statement in verse 28. How do they differ?

• What do you think Jesus would identify as keeping you from following him fully? What do you need to do?

The epitome of self-denial is Jesus in the garden of Gethsemane the night before his crucifixion. Self-denial is summed up in his prayer to God, "Not as I will, but as you will." That night he asked his friends to stay awake and pray with him. Just like in Jesus' agonizing dark night of the soul, those periods during which you wrestle with giving your will over to God are times when you need the support of friends the most.

Matthew 26:36-46

• What practices did Jesus model as he struggled with the ultimate act of self-denial?

• Whom would you want to surround you during a dark night of the soul?

the word on...
EVANGELISM

sunday *What Is Evangelism?*

_____

_____

_____

_____

_____

_____

_____

_____

_____

_____

_____

_____

Evangel means good news. The Christmas story of Christ's birth includes a powerful account of how ordinary shepherds became contagious ambassadors who shared the good news of Jesus Christ, or evangelized, after a personal encounter with him. When God's angel and heavenly host appeared to them, the shepherds found their way to the bedside of baby Jesus. Their faith in the good news of Christ, born to Earth to restore all humanity to relationship with God, motivated them to go and spread the good news to everyone they knew. God calls you, like the shepherds, to share your wonder and excitement about the good news of Jesus with others.

Luke 2:1-20

• Reread verses 16-20. What did the shepherds do after going and spreading the good news of Jesus? Why was this significant?

• Staying connected to the presence of Christ helps you stay spiritually energized. How do you practice this?

Today's simple story from the life of Jesus is a powerful illustration of how the miraculous touch of Christ can bring what was formerly "dead" to life once more. Jesus, filled with compassion for a grieving mother, brought life to her circumstances through his presence, and powerful touch to where her brokenness lay. The good news of Jesus you share with those around you who are trapped in "dead" situations, dead relationships, or the deadly consequences of poor decisions has the power to bring new life and hope. Let the compassionate heart and message of Christ, the "evangel," extend through you to touch others.

Luke 7:11-17

• Filled with awe and praise for God, how far did eyewitnesses to this miracle spread the good news?

• Whom do you know who needs the compassionate good news of Jesus for new life? What steps will you take to share the good news with that person?

Jesus Christ has the ultimate authority over any and all "demons" that threaten to overcome or destroy your life. But you must be willing to meet Jesus and surrender yourself fully to his supernatural life transformation. The man in today's story had struggled for years, yet after coming to meet Jesus he finally experienced freedom and peace. Jesus instructed him to go and tell the good news through sharing his story of deliverance. Your personal story of how new life in Christ delivered you from the struggles and disobedience of your past is a potent tool God can use to bring spiritual truth to others.

Luke 8:26-39

• According to verse 36, who were also "evangelists" of the life-transforming power of Jesus in addition to the man who met Jesus? Why?

• What is your story of what Jesus has done for you? Prepare yourself to share it with others.

wednesday *Is Evangelism For Special Occasions Only?*

As a follower of Jesus, you are sent out every day into your daily circumstances to be a living, breathing witness or "evangelist" of God's good news through Jesus. You may evangelize others through your loving actions, through serving those in need, through sharing your personal story of life transformation, or through explaining how God can meet us at any point of need or brokenness through Jesus. You may, at times, have the opportunity to guide someone as he or she makes a decision to accept Christ as Lord and Savior. The call of a believer to the lifestyle of an evangelist is not to "bludgeon" others with the gospel but to bring the joyous message of life and hope through both actions and words.

Luke 10:1-24

• When Jesus sent out his disciples to be evangelists, what were some of the key instructions he gave them? What results did they report?

• Verse 20 contains a crucial truth Jesus wants his followers to keep in mind. What is it?

thursday *What Effect Does One Person's Spiritual Conversion Have On Others?*

When those who are in desperate need of answers and healing call out for help, Jesus is always quick to respond. But those who want spiritual transformation and wholeness through Christ must be willing to surrender their issues and name their need. In your role as an evangelist (bringing the good news of the gospel to others), remember the technique Jesus demonstrated with the blind beggar. Know that as you assist individuals to connect with Jesus, others will also be influenced.

Luke 18:35-43

• What were the steps that Jesus took to help the blind beggar experience healing and spiritual conversion? What was the ripple effect on the others around the beggar?

• Think about what the blind beggar said he wanted. Do you want the same thing—enough to follow Jesus completely?

Expressing gratefulness to Christ for the healing transformation of your life is a powerful tool of evangelism. When Jesus healed ten lepers, only one thanked Jesus, "praising God in a loud voice" so that many others could hear. The author of Psalm 86 wrote about a variety of blessings and benefits he received through his relationship with God and promised to praise God with his whole heart. A key component of sharing the good news of faith is expressing thanks for what Jesus has done for you.

Luke 17:11-19 and Psalm 86:1-13

• Why do you think the other nine lepers didn't turn back to thank Jesus?

• Like the leper, for what can you "turn back" to thank Christ today?

According to Romans 1:19-20, the divine design and beauty of nature all around you bears witness to God's miraculous works. How powerful it is to realize that even creation reflects the "evangel" or good news of God! The unique beauty of God's world can serve as a reminder that you, as another part of God's creation, are also called to be an evangelist in both words and actions. Today's psalm celebrates both God's handiwork in how the world has been created and the inspiration of God's word, the Bible, in helping believers develop an obedient, contagious lifestyle.

Psalm 19:1-14

• How does the beauty of creation help inspire your awareness of God's good news of love?

• Do the "words of your mouth" to others about God match up with the true "meditations of your heart"? What might enhance this?

RUTH

JUDGES

NEHEMIAH

EZRA

ISAIAH

SONG of SOL.

JEREMIAH

sunday *Is Godly Wisdom Countercultural To Worldly Wisdom?*

According to the Bible, one set of visitors to the manger of baby Jesus was the magi. These individuals were likely from a set of priests in Persia known for their knowledge of religion and astrology. When they arrived in Jerusalem following a star, King Herod tried to circumvent any political uproar their search might cause by attempting to form an alliance with them. But after the magi were provided wisdom from God through a dream, they chose to be obedient and safely return home another way rather than obey the instructions of the king.

Matthew 2:1-23

• What did the magi do (verse 11) that prepared them to receive God's direction to choose a different route?

• When you desire the countercultural wisdom of God's guidance, how can you likewise prepare yourself to "hear" it?

RUTH

NEHEMIA

JEREM

JONAH

TIMOTHY

As the magi learned, following God's wisdom and guidance brings safety and purpose that the advice of the world cannot provide. The countercultural approach of aligning everything in your life—your thinking, your choices, your relationships, your faith, and even your physical health—according to the wisdom of God is the only path to true transformation. In the book of Proverbs, the benefits of embracing God's wisdom are clearly detailed.

Proverbs 4:1-27

• According to verses 7-9, why is God's wisdom so important? What might it "cost" you to pursue it?

• From today's reading, what do you consider the most important benefit of seeking God's wisdom?

Godly wisdom begins with the understanding and acceptance of the sacrifice of Jesus for your sins, that you might receive new life in God. By going against the grain of the world and the ideas of our contemporary culture and instead seeking relationship with God through Jesus Christ, you will find wisdom that brings a dramatic contrast to the human thinking around you. Jesus is indeed the embodiment of the deep wisdom of God, as explained by the Apostle Paul.

1 Corinthians 1:18-31

• In verse 18, how does Paul describe the message of the cross as seen by the world versus how it is seen by Christians?

• What are some ways our culture defines "wisdom" that in God's eyes are foolishness?

wednesday

Faithfully living out God's wisdom will bring you a "life makeover" that others will not always be able to understand or believe. God's wisdom through Jesus constantly brought him new insights into Scripture teachings as well as miraculous power beyond his ordinary circumstances. God's storeroom of wisdom provides believers with both timeless truths and corresponding wise application for daily living.

Matthew 13:47-58

• Where and how did Jesus get the wisdom that made his former hometown neighbors marvel? Have you ever received this reaction?

• What is a new insight of wisdom your own Bible study has recently brought you?

thursday

Like the magi taking the redirected route home so long ago, following the countercultural path of godly wisdom home to God will take you on a path that may seem radically different from what others expect. The wisdom of life in Christ is not about "show" or fulfilling rules set up by humans. Instead, it is about surrendering to the headship of Christ and his lifestyle.

Colossians 2:1-23

• In Christ are hidden "all treasures of wisdom and knowledge" (verse 3). Name several examples.

• What did Paul write that some believers were focusing on instead of Christ's wisdom? Do you struggle with any of these distractions?

Conventional worldly wisdom can lead you to think that doing what you want, when you want, is the best approach. But praying and obeying God's wise timing will lead you into the blessing and peace of God's best will. Whether in good times or challenging times, trusting God's direction and wise time frame, rather than your own, will guide your path and help you mature spiritually.

Ecclesiastes 3:1-14

• How is Ecclesiastes 3:14 a statement about God's wisdom?

• Reread verses 2-8. For which of these situations are you most seeking God's wisdom and timing right now?

Symptoms of godly wisdom in the life of a believer will result in a change of behavior, not just of thinking. When you make a shift from following conventional wisdom into embracing the countercultural approach of the wisdom in Christ, it activates your behavior and guides you into a faith-filled lifestyle. Even more, those who walk in godly wisdom become ambassadors of the peace of Christ, the One who is known as the Prince of Peace.

James 3:13-18

• Make a list of the symptoms of worldly wisdom versus those of godly wisdom.

• Which symptom of godly wisdom do you most desire to develop? What will you need to change or surrender?

the word on...
A NEW SONG

What Is The Best Way For Me To Begin The New Year?

The eve of a new year is always a great time to evaluate your life and relationships, and it is also a great time to consider the wonder and majesty of the God you serve. God, as Creator, is always making things new. As the new year begins, you too should start out with a new song in your heart for the God who loves and takes care of you.

Psalm 33

• List the reasons that the psalmist gave God praise in today's reading. Which of these resounds in your heart also?

• For what do you need to thank God in the year that is ending? What "new song" do you need to sing to God as you begin this new year?

Not only is God the creator of new things, God is a God of new chances. One of the most striking characteristics seen between God and the Israelite people in the Old Testament is the continual opportunity for repentance, grace, and restoration. And in Jesus' teaching and ministry you see God's great desire for everyone to return to right relationship no matter what they have done or how many times they have failed.

Isaiah 55:6-9 and Luke 15:11-32

• What are the characteristics of the Father in the story of the prodigal son? Which means the most to you?

• How has God shown you love and mercy this year even when you didn't deserve it?

The God of another chance is also the God who restores you to new life and power. You no longer have to live in sin and defeat; in Christ you are blessed and given renewed life so that you can live to honor God. Christ also honors you by commissioning you to take this wonderful message of life to those around you who are broken.

Romans 6:1-14
and 2 Corinthians 5:17-21

• According to Romans 6, how do you break from the bonds of sinful living?

• What will you do in this new year to serve as Christ's ambassador?

wednesday

_____

_____

_____

_____

_____

_____

_____

_____

_____

_____

Everyone goes through times of spiritual struggle or fatigue, whether from persecution, personal struggles, physical issues, or spiritual burnout. But God promises to renew you and give you continual strength if you will just rely on the Holy Spirit day by day. Even when things around you are seemingly in turmoil, fix your eyes and faith on God and you will become rejuvenated and refreshed.

Isaiah 40:25-31
and 2 Corinthians 4:7-18

• What does Isaiah advise in order to become renewed in strength? How about Paul in the 2 Corinthians reading?

• How much time each day do you allow God the opportunity to renew your life and spirit?

thursday

_____

_____

_____

_____

_____

_____

_____

_____

_____

The same God who brings you into a new life and service also at times desires to send you in new and fruitful directions. To become the true hands and feet of Jesus you must always be open to the guidance of God and receptive to where God might send you. Because Paul was continually open to God's leading, he was able to reach whole new communities and cultures for Christ.

Acts 16:1-15
and 2 Thessalonians 3:1-5

• What was Paul's reaction to both the impeding and the prompting of the Holy Spirit in his ministry?

• How can you become more open to God's guidance leading in your life?

Even though you are called as a servant of Jesus to bring the kingdom of God into this broken world, God will in the end totally renew all things including both the heavens and the earth. As you read today's passages, let them inspire you to live with purity as well as give you hope that sin, death, and all evil will some day be defeated by God and that you will inherit this new kingdom as God's child.

2 Peter 3:8-14
and Revelation 21:1-7

• Why is the Lord patient in the process of ultimately renewing all things (2 Peter 3:8-9)?

• How does knowing God's eventual, ultimate plan inspire you to live with purity and in service to God?

Because you serve a wonderful God who brings you new life and purpose, choose an attitude of gratitude, worship, and praise on a daily basis. It is in lifting up the name of God that you become filled with the joy and inspiration that will keep you on the right path and in the direction God leads. Sing to the Lord your new song each day, and watch your life be filled with God's presence.

Psalm 96:1-13

• Make a list of the characteristics of God in this psalm.

• Make your own list of the things for which you want to thank and praise God.

the word on...
MY SAVIOR

sunday *Why Do I Need A Savior?*

_____

_____

_____

_____

_____

_____

_____

_____

_____

_____

_____

_____

The spiritual DNA from your spiritual ancestors, Adam and Eve, has resulted in internal brokenness and separation from God. No human is able to overcome this ingrained power of sin on his or her own. Jesus died for you personally to take on your sin, address your brokenness, and restore you to an intimate relationship with God. Because of this great gift, you are to be active in the reconciliation process with others.

Romans 5:6–11
and 2 Corinthians 5:17-6:2

• What words does Paul use to describe individuals before they know Christ (Romans 5:6, 8,10)?

• How has Christ made a difference in your life?

A relationship with Jesus is a work in progress. Although you are reconciled to God, your human nature will be pulled toward old thoughts, attitudes, and behavior patterns, leading you to sin. God's call is to obedience, but all followers of Christ need help to fully obey. Through the power, ongoing presence, and advocacy of Jesus you can acknowledge your sin, receive forgiveness, and freely move forward in your transformation process. Jesus is your "wonderful counselor," as the Scriptures say.

1 John 2:1-2 and John 14:15-21

• Whom does God provide to advocate, counsel, and guide you in your daily walk (1 John 2:1 and John 14:17)?

• Take time to ask God for guidance and counsel for any specific concern you have today.

Jesus, described in Scripture as the Prince of Peace and present in your life through the Holy Spirit, brings peace that is almost inexplicable. This is not the peace the world offers; this is an inner tranquility that releases you from fear and anxiety and gives you confidence in God's ultimate control no matter what is happening. Teamed with Jesus, you can find deep rest for your soul.

Matthew 11:25-30
and John 14:25-31

• How is the peace Jesus gives different from what the world provides?

• What burden do you need to give to Jesus in order to experience his rest?

wednesday

_____
_____
_____
_____
_____
_____
_____
_____
_____
_____
_____

Rather than an uncertainty ("I sure hope this will happen"), hope in Christ is the inner certainty that God is at work accomplishing God's will in your life. Even if the circumstances surrounding you are painful or disturbing, your hope as a believer asserts that God is good, powerful, and working on your behalf for the best outcome. Hope is based on the foundation of God's love poured out for you through Jesus.

1 Peter 1:3-9 and Romans 5:1-5

• In what are you to rejoice? Why?

• Write a prayer of praise to God for what is happening in your life because of the hope you have in Jesus.

thursday

_____
_____
_____
_____
_____
_____
_____
_____
_____
_____
_____

The meaning of salvation is health, wellness, and wholeness. God is not just about saving souls for eternity. God wants the best for believers now and becomes invested in an ongoing process of healing and transformation in each believer's life. Jesus has the power to heal, is willing to respond compassionately to your needs, and will keep touching lives until they are fully restored.

Mark 1:40-45 and 8:22-26

• When the blind man in Mark 8 was not completely healed, what did Jesus do? Why do you think this healing took place in stages?

• What ongoing issue(s) do you need to have Jesus touch again to move you toward complete healing?

Jesus promises to meet all your needs, both spiritually and physically. Just as God provided manna in the wilderness for the Israelites, Jesus, the bread of life, will fill your spiritual hunger and thirst. He said he will sustain everyone who chooses to "remain in me," and will ensure that life will be full, continually growing and meaningful.

John 6:32-40

• What did Jesus say would happen to those who come to him as the bread of life?

• Give an example of how Jesus has satisfied your spiritual hunger or thirst.

Based on his death and resurrection, Jesus has the right to be Lord—the absolute authority over your life. Jesus is not interested in your performance or your living up to external standards. His call is for you to give up seeking approval and accolades from other people and to seek only to do the will of God. Submission and obedience reflect the lifestyle of those who have Jesus as Lord of their lives.

Matthew 7:21-29
and Romans 14:7-9

• According to Jesus, what characterizes the person who authentically can call him Lord?

• How is your foundation in Jesus? Are you like the wise person or the foolish person?